THE COFFEE TABLE BOOK OF

THE COFFEE TABLE BOOK OF DOOM

Steven Appleby & Art Lester

FACING THE FUTURE:

Warning

Perhaps by the time you read this book
some of the Doom scenarios included will no longer be
global threats. Maybe the human race will have
acted together to contain greenhouse gas production
and tree felling. Or they will have developed a
laser shield to deflect incoming asteroids.
Perhaps not.

All the facts and theories in this book have been checked
as thoroughly as possible. We humbly apologise
for any errors which may have crept in.
After all, we are human – as we assume you are.

The authors wish to express their heartfelt gratitude
to those who have made this book possible through their contributions,
their expertise and, perhaps above all, their forbearance.
They include: Pete Bishop, Lloyd Clater, Rosemary Davidson, Nick Battey,
Simon Rhodes, and Jo Unwin, our agent.
Special thanks to Gilly Fraser, Nicola Sherring and family.

First published in 2011 by Square Peg

A member of
The Random House Group Limited
20 Vauxhall Bridge Road
London
SW1V 2SA

www.randomhouse.co.uk

Printed on paper not made from timber
No tree has been harmed in the creation of this book
and Doom has not been encouraged

Set in Century Gothic & Trebuchet

ISBN 9780224086950

Printed and bound in China by C&C Offset Printing Co Limited

The Random House Group Limited supports The Forest Stewardship Council®(FSC®), the
leading international forest certification organisation. Our books carrying the FSC label
are printed on FSC® certified paper. FSC is the only forest certification scheme
endorsed by the leading environmental organisations, including Greenpeace. Our
paper procurement policy can be found at www.randomhouse.co.uk/environment

This book is dedicated to the Earth.
We hope that its end will be exciting for
anyone who happens to be
passing by and stops to watch.

Dear fellow mortal,

Imagine that you're sitting on your sofa leafing through this book, when you feel an odd vibration. Ripples start to shiver across the surface of your teacup. Puzzled, you strain your ears. Then you hear a distant rumbling. Barely audible to begin with, the noise grows louder. And nearer. The sound is unfamiliar at first, but then you realise what it is.

Hoofbeats.

Don't go to your window and peer through the curtains. Don't tempt the horsemen of the Apocalypse by showing your face.

Doom is no longer far off in the distant future. It could arrive as early as Tuesday morning.

And there's nothing you can do except read on...

Yours anxiously,

The authors

SOME WAYS THE WORLD MIGHT END

i – Baked

ii – Boiled

iii – Fried

iv – Frozen

v – Squished

vi – Smashed

vii – Squeezed

viii – Sucked-dry

ix – Bounced

x – Burnt

xi – Toast...

DOOM — What's That?

Do we even have to ask? Everyone knows what Doom is. We've never actually seen it, and lots of predictions anticipating it have failed to materialise, but it's been with us since the cave days. It was there with us when we hid under the covers as children, and it flashes into view every time we switch on the evening news.

fig a — CURTAINS

Don't look out!

Everyone knows: it's curtains.

Here's a dictionary definition:

> **Doom:** (dū:m), noun.
> Fate or destiny, especially adverse; unavoidable ill fortune; ruin; an unfavourable judgement or sentence; the Last Judgement, at the end of the world.

It seems we all know about Doom because, as the definition confirms, it's our destiny; it's unavoidable. That's why religions are full of it. In theology, talking about it is called eschatology, or the knowledge of the 'end times'. Because it's linked to the Last Judgement, Christian, Jewish and Muslim holy books describe it as a final pay-off for unbelievers. Infidels will all be wiped out – usually horribly – while the good guys will be saved. If you're a certain type of fundamentalist, you're just waiting to be 'raptured', or maybe beamed aboard a spaceship. But even modern, secular types have doom anxiety. You bought this book, didn't you?

For nearly everybody, it's all about guilt. When things are going along pretty well, it's natural to think they can't last. Walking along a pavement on a sunny day is an invitation for someone to drop a grand piano on your head. We feel that something must be wrong with the way we're living. Using all that energy, buying a second home while some people are sleeping in cardboard cartons, eating strawberries at Christmas dinner. It's all too obvious: we're heading for a fall. Aren't we?

CARVING THE
CHRISTMAS STRAWBERRY

You're asking for it! ?

We cling to our Doom anxiety like a Linus blanket. Maybe we know that living without Doom would be like a football match without a final whistle, a sandwich with no bread, a murder mystery with no villain. Unimaginable. Worse: boring.

So we look fearfully at the skies, listen for rumours of new dread diseases and nuclear accidents from behind the sofa, and take an aspirin every morning. We know that if there was no Doom, we'd be forced to invent it.

How will the end happen?

Read this book!

THE END IS COMING

DOOM

How Do We Know Doom is Coming?

Prophesies. We can be sure that prophets have always had a stab at predicting the end of the world. Most of these have been lost in time, but the present count of known prophesies stands at 147.*

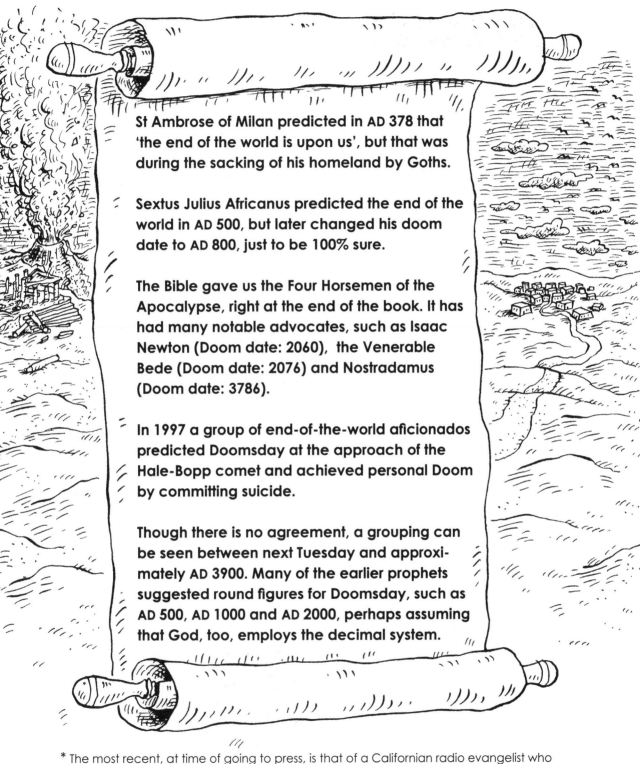

St Ambrose of Milan predicted in AD 378 that 'the end of the world is upon us', but that was during the sacking of his homeland by Goths.

Sextus Julius Africanus predicted the end of the world in AD 500, but later changed his doom date to AD 800, just to be 100% sure.

The Bible gave us the Four Horsemen of the Apocalypse, right at the end of the book. It has had many notable advocates, such as Isaac Newton (Doom date: 2060), the Venerable Bede (Doom date: 2076) and Nostradamus (Doom date: 3786).

In 1997 a group of end-of-the-world aficionados predicted Doomsday at the approach of the Hale-Bopp comet and achieved personal Doom by committing suicide.

Though there is no agreement, a grouping can be seen between next Tuesday and approximately AD 3900. Many of the earlier prophets suggested round figures for Doomsday, such as AD 500, AD 1000 and AD 2000, perhaps assuming that God, too, employs the decimal system.

* The most recent, at time of going to press, is that of a Californian radio evangelist who predicted 'rapture' of true believers on 21 May 2011, to be followed by world destruction in October of the same year.

TIMELINE SHOWING WHEN THE WORLD IS PREDICTED TO END...

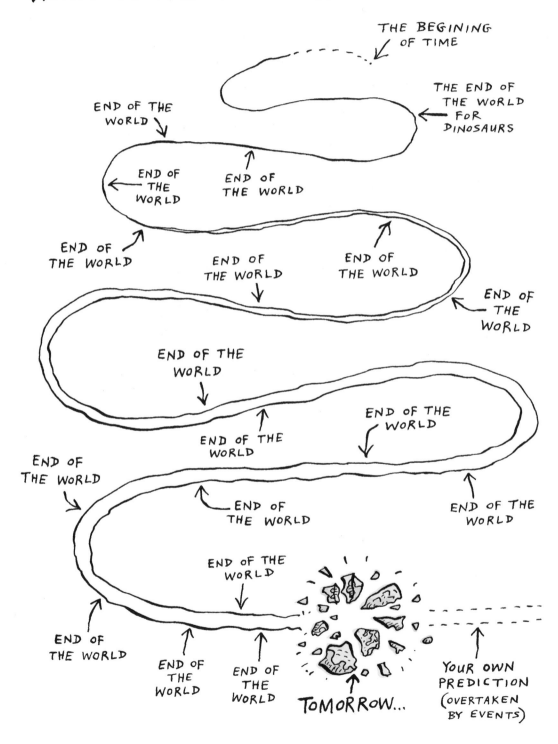

Our next date with Doom appears to be in December 2012. That's according to the ancient Mayan calendar, which ends then after a period of civilisation lasting 5,125 years. Strangely, this appears to concur with a prediction made by St Malachy in 1143, who said the world would end during the tenure of the 112th future pope. The current pontiff, Benedict XVI, is the 111th, and he's 83 years old.

21 December 2012. Write that date in your diary.

Science. Once Galileo started messing around with lenses and had the first good look at the stars, we began to hear from astronomers and other scientists. They've been identifying ways we might end ever since.

The white-coated prophets of the laboratories have produced dozens of nightmare scenarios. These range from hideous new diseases to collisions with lumps of rock in space and invisible death rays.

Eerily, many of their most recent predictions tend to point to the year 2012.

Intuition. We human beings are the only creatures that have a sense of time.

So we just *know*.

You might think that the enterprise of science, with its method and its facts, would inoculate us against the most extravagant doomsday obsessions. But it doesn't. If anything, it just gives us more to worry about.

Scientific American, September 2010

Contents

197

Asteroid Strike

What are the odds that Earth will someday be impacted by an object from space?

100%.

In fact, every day over half a million pieces of rock from space enter the Earth's atmosphere. Of course, most of these are harmlessly burned away by the

atmosphere and become 'shooting stars'. But some will get through and wind up as paperweights on the desks of scientists.

A bigger chunk of rock (a swimming pool-sized object) sailed between the Earth and the Moon in the summer of 2010. We didn't know about that one until it had passed. Somewhat larger objects of 100 metres (like a football pitch) would destroy cities. There are known to be more than 100,000 of these in our cosmic neighbourhood.

Recently an object called Apophys, with a diameter of 270 metres, has turned up. At first it was thought that there might be a collision with us sometime in 2024, but it now seems that a near miss is more likely. What is a problem is something called a 'gravitational keyhole', a zone of just a few metres that can

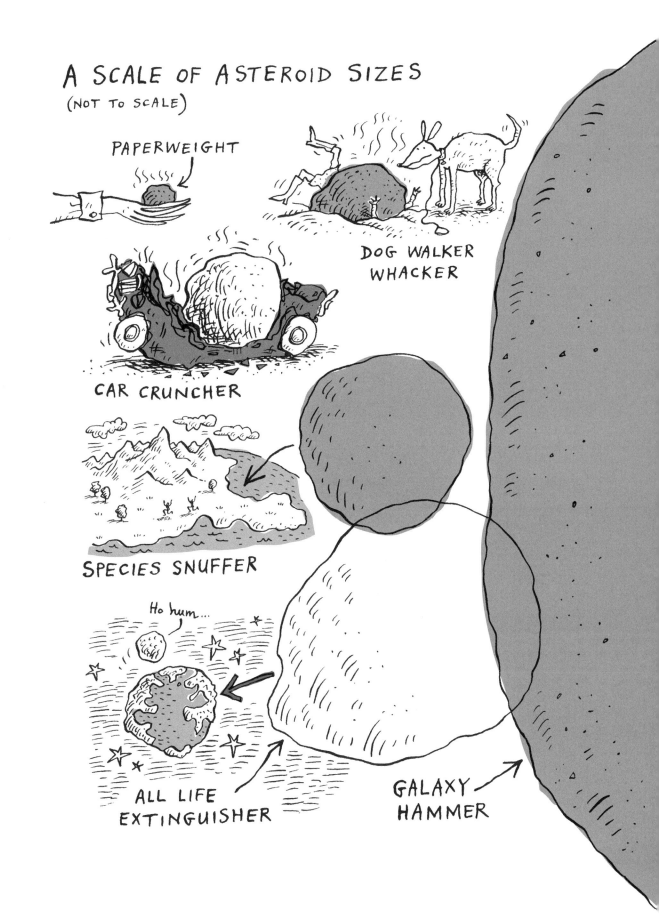

alter the trajectory of an object passing through it. That would mean a return of Apophys in the year 2036. And next time it might not miss.

IN ORDER TO FULLY APPRECIATE THE LIKELIHOOD OF THE EARTH BEING HIT BY LARGE ASTEROIDS, WHY NOT REPLICATE THE SOLAR SYSTEM IN **YOUR OWN HOME!** YOU REPRESENT THE EARTH...

SIMPLY:

i – HANG CROCKERY, PANS AND OTHER ITEMS FROM YOUR CEILING.

ii – WALK ABOUT BRISKLY WITH YOUR EYES CLOSED.

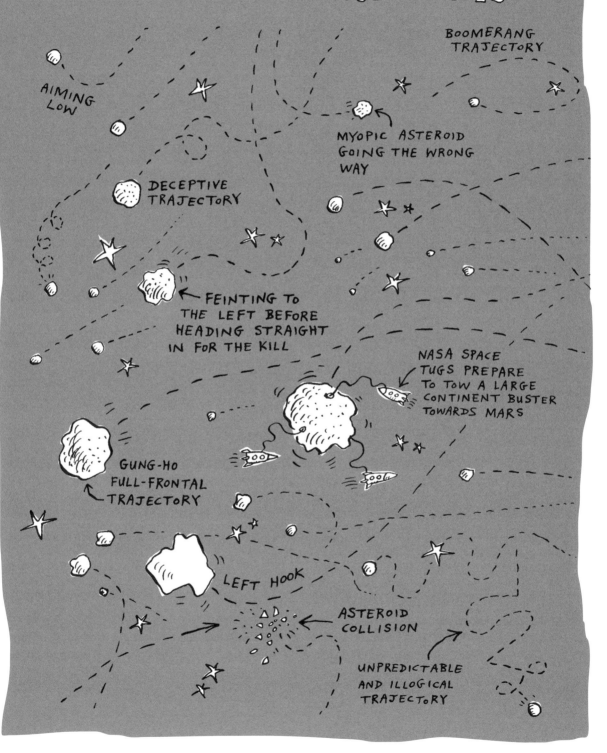

If Apophys enters the atmosphere it will be travelling at 50,000 mph and explode with the force of 30,000 Hiroshima bombs, making a crater about the size of New York. It will generate high-speed winds that will flatten buildings in much of the planet and may raise the temperature of the air to an unbearable level. Massive tsunamis would affect all coasts, and the likelihood of an artificial winter is great.

According to the Task Force on Near Earth Objects set up in 2000, there are about 1,000 known nearby asteroids with diameters of greater than one kilometre, any one of which is capable of causing global destruction. These big lumps of rock are known as 'species busters'. One of these, called 1950 DA, has a good chance of hitting us in 2880, according to *Science* magazine.

What can we do about it? Scientists have proposed deflecting Apophys with nuclear weapons, blowing it up, and even inventing a 'space tug' equipped with plasma engines. Then there is the 'Yarkovsky effect', in which focused solar heat causes the asteroid to shift its trajectory. So far nobody has got further than the theoretical stage, so nobody knows if any of this will work.

Experts say we still don't really know what's out there. An impact could happen at any time.

Like tomorrow.

Gamma Wave Pulse

Earth is a sitting duck for pulses of destructive energy that come from so far away in the cosmos that we can't even detect the source.

Gamma rays, the most powerful form of radiation, are created from the decay of radioactive material. Sometimes they appear as the result of a supernova explosion, such as that of the Crab Nebula, which lit up the sky in 1054. When stars explode, or when black holes get tetchy, they emit this super-strong radiation in pulses that last for fractions of a second to several minutes.

These pulses travel at the speed of light through space and pass through every solid object they encounter.
Unlike visible light, they cannot be seen or their images captured in mirrors.

Because they have the shortest wavelength of any known form of radiation, they are the strongest. A burst can release more energy in ten seconds than the Sun will emit in ten billion years. The rays kill human cells, which is why they are used in cancer therapies. If a gamma wave burst were to strike the Earth, much of the protective ozone layer would be stripped away, leaving all life susceptible to ultraviolet and other harmful forms of radiation from our own Sun.

Gamma wave pulses are not rare. According to NASA, they are continually occurring in various part of the universe, popping like flashbulbs every few seconds. Optimistically, astrophysicists until recently have believed that such a flash only happens within our galaxy every few million years.

However, the explosion of the small neutron star known as SGR 1806-20 in late 2004 was a surprise event that disrupted communications satellites and caused other effects still being argued in scientific circles (see page 187–6). Another surprise finding by glaciologists in 1987 of isotopes of beryllium-10 in ice samples showed that large waves of cosmic rays have impacted with Earth in much more recent history.

Still, it doesn't happen very often.

Does it?

ARTIST'S IMPRESSION
OF HOW GAMMA RAYS
CROSS THE UNIVERSE,
CAUSING EARTHQUAKES

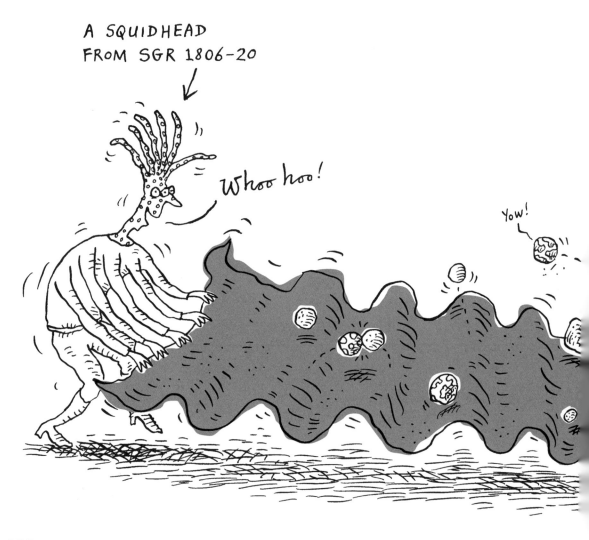

A SQUIDHEAD
FROM SGR 1806-20

Whoo hoo!

Yow!

Earthquakes from Outer Space

Can earthquakes start in outer space?

Some scientists are beginning to think so. When a star collapses into itself, huge amounts of energy in the form of gamma rays are released in fairly narrow bands. As they travel, gamma rays form gravitational surges that move faster than the rays themselves.

The earthquake of Boxing Day 2004 caused a huge tsunami in the Pacific that killed more than 240,000 people. By far the largest quake of modern times, it registered 9.4 on the Richter scale. Just 44 hours later, a gamma ray burst struck the Earth. This was over 100 times more powerful than any previously recorded instance. It temporarily changed the shape of the Earth's ionosphere and severely distorted radio signals.

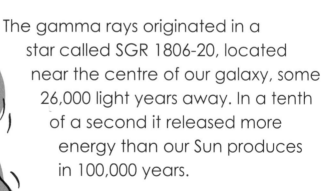

wheee!

The gamma rays originated in a star called SGR 1806-20, located near the centre of our galaxy, some 26,000 light years away. In a tenth of a second it released more energy than our Sun produces in 100,000 years.

Scientists speculate that the two events being so close together in time is more than coincidence. Because gamma rays are slowed by passing through electrons and space dust, the gravitational pulse would have hit the Earth at just about the time of the earthquake on 26 December.

It is now possible to identify fault lines where earthquakes are likely to occur, but it is still an inexact science to try to predict when they will happen. If their origin is thousands of light years away, we may never know until it is too late.

'If anything, the December 27, 2004 gamma ray burst shows us that we do not live in a peaceful celestial environment... Like the December 26th earthquake and the December 27th gamma ray burst, the next superwave will arrive unexpectedly. It will take us by surprise,' says Dr Paul La Violette of the Starburst Foundation.

Gravitational pulses don't just come from far away in the galaxy. Early in March 2011, scientists recorded a spectacular X-class solar flare within line of sight of the Earth. The colossal earthquake near Japan, with its resulting tsunami, hit just a matter of a few hours afterwards.

Contagion from Space

We are in danger of invasion from space. And the aliens are too tiny to see.

Microbes may travel huge stellar distances attached to comets, scientists now believe, and have almost certainly entered Earth's atmosphere. Because we have evolved without any prior contact with these tiny life forms, we would have no innate resistance to fall back on in the event of infection.

This real-life update of *The Day of the Triffids* enjoys the support of some noted astrobiologists. The recent discovery of microorganisms in the upper reaches of the atmosphere lends further credence to the existence of life from outer space.

Uh oh.
A disease
from space.

In fact, some believe that all life on Earth began when a comet or other astral body deposited microbial life on Earth nearly four billion years ago. This theory, known as panspermia, is defended by well-known scientists such as Professor Chandra Wickramasinghe, Director of the Cardiff Centre for Astrobiology.

HERE ARE SOME DISEASES FROM SPACE YOU MAY ALREADY BE FAMILIAR WITH:

i – SUSPICION.

ii – JEALOUSY.

iii – ANGER.

iv – LYING.

v – MORE LYING...

vi – AND EVEN MORE LYING.

vii – DOUBT.

viii – DEPRESSION.

ix – HONESTY.

It was previously believed that the harsh conditions of space, such as freezing and very high temperatures, lack of oxygen and gravity would make microbial life impossible outside the comfort zone of Earth or an Earth-like planet. But recent discoveries of life in extreme conditions on Earth have given a different picture.

In 1969, NASA recovered streptococcus mitis bacteria from a camera brought back from the moon by astronauts Pete Conrad and Alan L. Bean. The camera had been deposited there 30 months earlier by an unmanned space probe. Because of the rigorous precautions of the space programme, it is known that the camera was free of Earth organisms at the time of launch, so the conclusion is clear:

Germs can live on the Moon.

Even more frightening is the discovery that certain bacteria actually grow faster and get stronger in zero gravity. This might mean that the microorganisms that make it through would be even tougher to defeat than the Earth-born ones.

Assuming that antibiotics and antiviral drugs continue to work (see page 135–4), we can just about manage to avoid mass contagion from germs that share our evolutionary history.

But nobody ever thought that diseases might fall from the sky.

I'm contagious, earthlings.

Earth's Poles Reverse

The world is about to turn upside down.

CLONK

SATELLITE ORBITS ARE DISRUPTED

Scientists predict that a North/South pole reversal occurs every 300,000 years or so. It happens when the strength of the planet's magnetic field diminishes. In such times, what has been the focal point of magnetic compasses gets disordered, finally flipping over, making things work in reverse. Migrating birds get lost. Navigation becomes problematic for everybody, including our satellites, ships and planes.

The present strength of the magnetic field is far lower than in historically verifiable times. Some scientists believe that the 'magnetic deficit' accounts for the fact that there are fewer large land animals than in past eras. The dinosaurs thrived during hefty magnetic times.

Our magnetic field is now weak. Very weak. Despite the direst predictions of the lunatic fringe, if the magnetic poles reverse, the Sun

BIRDS FLY UPSIDE DOWN & BACKWARDS

will not start rising in the west, and the hot core of the planet is not going to burst its container. At least, most scientists don't think so.

SHIPS GET LOST

But what could actually happen is nearly as bad.

When the Earth's magnetic field gets weak enough to shift poles, the protective envelope that shields us from cosmic rays gets less effective. The atmosphere gets thinner. The planet becomes even more susceptible to the huge emissions of ultraviolet light, X-rays and gamma rays from the Sun. Radiation-generated illnesses such as melanoma increase. Communications systems are disordered, and in a severe enough instance, all digital technology could be rendered ineffective.

As if that wasn't bad enough, our local star flips its magnetic field once every 11 years, and when that happens, huge solar storms increase and produce even more dangerous radiation than usual.

Croydon should be just over the next ridge.

MRS BELLOW'S SENSE OF DIRECTION LETS HER DOWN

When is the next expected pole reversal for the Sun? 2012.

False Vacuum Event

Space is a giant vacuum. One big void, full of absolutely nothing.

False.

Theoretical physicists have uncovered a new and worrying possibility: what if the vacuum we know as space isn't really a vacuum at all, but simply an area of minimum density? And what if the universe, very big indeed if not actually infinite, does contain bona fide vacuums? Some theories suggest that it probably does, give or take a few trillion misbehaving quantum particles.

If such a vacuum got into our cosmic neighbourhood, according to physicists like S. Coleman and F. de Luccia, it would arrive at nearly the speed of light and gobble up the solar system instantaneously. There would be no warning, no sirens or flashing red lights, no instructions on building fallout shelters. We would simply disappear as if we had never existed. This is called a 'vacuum metastability event', but it's really just another word for curtains.

Imagine that our universe is a bubble of air rising towards the surface throughout the history of the universe. Imagine then what happens when we finally arrive at the surface.

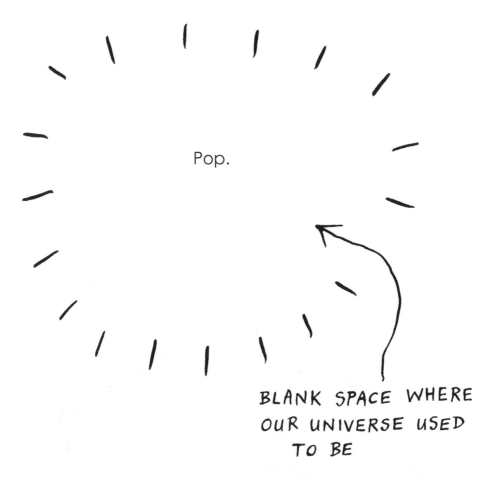

Pop.

BLANK SPACE WHERE OUR UNIVERSE USED TO BE

As Coleman and de Luccia say:

...after vacuum decay, not only is life as we know it impossible, so is chemistry as we know it. However, one [used to be able to] draw stoic comfort from the possibility that perhaps in the course of time the new vacuum would sustain, if not life as we know it, at least some structures capable of knowing joy. This possibility has now been eliminated.

(International Journal of Theoretical Physics, Vol. 45, No. 12)

Solar Storm

By the time you finish reading this page, we could have sunk from Digital Age to Stone Age.

Eight minutes. That's how long it takes light, gamma and X-rays to travel to the Earth from the Sun.

My digital solar flare detector has started counting down to its own destruction.

NEE NAW NEE NAW NEE NAW NEE NAW...

Worried scientists report that the Sun has a regular timetable of intense magnetic disturbances, when huge flares containing light, gamma and X-rays surge outward from the surface. Some of these will reach Earth if we are unlucky enough to be facing the wrong side of the Sun.

During four summer days in 1859, the Sun erupted with huge solar flares. Telegraph lines caught fire and in some cases burned down buildings. Sparks leapt from poles all over the United States and Europe. Some telegraph terminals seemed to go on emitting messages by themselves. The sky was electrified, with an aurora-borealis-style display visible in many parts of the temperate zones. It was so bright that people got up and had breakfast in the middle of the night.

In 2010, solar flares were becoming more active and frequent. In April, a Galaxy 15 satellite was disabled, and has now become an uncommunicative 'zombie' orbiting the Earth. In the further flares of 1 August, almost the entire Earth-facing side of the Sun erupted. A C3-class solar eruption caused large-scale shaking of the solar corona, radio bursts and a coronal mass ejection.

NASA has warned that a new solar cycle is beginning, and during 2012 will be at its strongest. If the disturbances are severe enough, all electrical grids will be affected, wiping out power networks. Telephones, cashpoints and air travel will cease functioning instantly. Computers will be destroyed. Water supplies will be cut off, leaving the populace without any of the life-supporting systems on which they now rely. The situation would last for weeks or months. The possibilities for civil unrest and disease are too dire to consider.

Stone Age people had options to deal with an Earth bare of modern services. We don't.

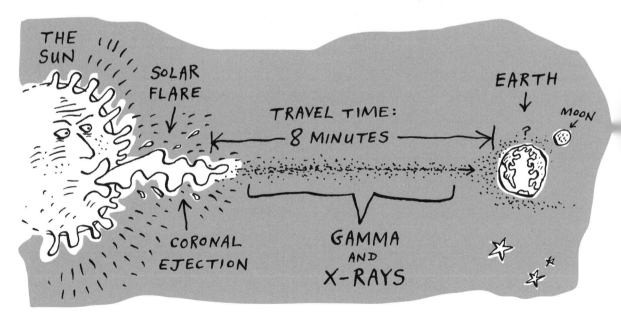

Alien Invasion

Ever since the time of H. G. Wells, we've been looking over our shoulders.

Little green men haven't turned up yet, as far as we know, but UFO enthusiasts all over the world would beg to differ. The photographs of the Roswell incident, complete with the supine body of an extraterrestrial visitor, continue to intrigue, despite years of official debunking. It seems that we still expect to meet ET at any moment.

Projections of encounters of the third kind fall into two categories. In the first, the aliens are not just more scientifically advanced – they are better beings than we are. Their purpose is to help, or at least benignly study, earthlings. Some apocalyptic visions include the 'rapture' of humanity into spacecraft for a new and better life. One such group, followers of the Hale–Bopp comet sect, were willing to drink cyanide squash in 1997 in order to meet intergalactic saviours of the human race.

The second group is more inclined to believe that any space invaders would do so for selfish reasons, either to occupy or to otherwise exploit Earth's resources. These cosmic bad guys seem to be just ahead in popular films.

Meanwhile, physicists tell us that the whole idea is probably absurd. They point out that the universe is a pretty big place, and that travel between stars – even at or approaching the speed of light – would take too long. Sci-fi writers get around this detail by envisioning 'warp drives' and 'wormholes' that

would make contact easier. But advances in mathematics and astrophysics have offered a new possibility of contact and maybe invasion from somewhere else.

Another dimension.

Ever since Einstein's general theory of relativity turned conventional physics on its axis, there has been the possibility of dimensions beyond the three we are aware of, plus time, a fourth. The more deeply we delve into the

UFOs ~ THE PROOF IS EVERYWHERE!

JUST TAKE A LOOK AT THIS...

A FLYING SAUCER UTILISING ITS CLOAKING DEVICE

A FLOTILLA OF FIGHTER ROCKETS USING INVISIBILITY SHIELDS

A VAST SPACESHIP DISGUISED TO LOOK LIKE AN EVERYDAY OBJECT

ALIENS IN LANDING PODS FITTED WITH MIMICRY REFLECTORS

171

workings of the universe, the more new dimensions turn up. String theory, which – at least for now – holds the high ground, has come up with eight or nine dimensions that we would not be aware of without mathematics. We would be no more able to see these dimensions than hear a dog whistle, because we don't have the sensory equipment.

Which all means that it's at least theoretically possible that we are sharing space and time with other beings, one of whom might have come up with a way to slip from their dimension into ours. Not intergalactic visitors, then.

Inter-dimensional ones.

Don't stop looking over your shoulder just yet.

A GUIDE TO SOME COMMON CREATURES FROM OTHER DIMENSIONS YOU SHOULD WATCH OUT FOR:

NOTE ~ THEY CAN REMAIN UTTERLY STILL FOR LONG PERIODS TO LULL YOU INTO A FALSE SENSE OF SECURITY.

RICH TEA

USED → TISSUE

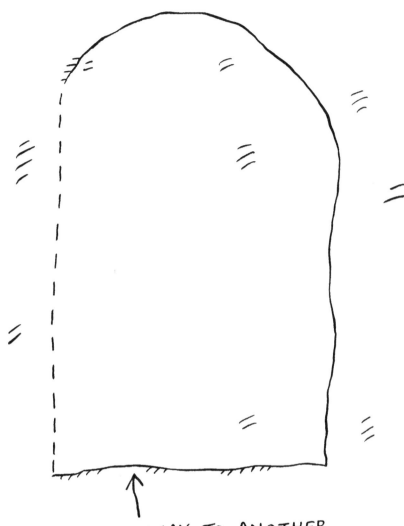

DOORWAY TO ANOTHER
DIMENSION. WHATEVER
YOU DO, **DON'T** CUT ALONG
THE THICK BLACK LINES
& FOLD OPEN ALONG DOTTED
LINE. GOD ONLY KNOWS
WHAT TERRIFYING CREATURE
MIGHT COME THROUGH!

Death of the Solar System

There are lots of ways the world might end. Some are more likely, others less so. But there is one Doom scenario on the horizon that is certain, total, and will bring about the end of everything we know.

A solar supernova.

Astrophysicists calculate that a star like our own has a life of about ten billion years. Ours is middle-aged, about halfway there. At some point during the next five billion years, in the space of a few seconds, the core of the Sun will collapse in on itself, explode and, for a brief instant, shine at a billion times its present brightness. It will be visible several galaxies away for a short time, then become a neutron star.

As it expands in its initial phase, it will devour Mercury and Venus. We won't mind, of course, because we will long since have vaporised. We won't be aware of being sucked into the black hole the Sun leaves in its wake, and being compressed into an unimaginably small space.

The astrophysicists can only offer us a tiny reassurance. This total end of everything isn't due for quite a while. Even if their theories do change every few years, they know pretty much everything about the universe.

Don't they?

THE LIFE CYCLE OF OUR SUN

OUR SUN AS A SKITTISH, YOUNG STAR. OPTIMISTIC AND EAGER.

THE TEENAGE SUN. A BIT BORED AND KNOW-IT-ALL.

IN ITS 'TWENTIES' AND 'THIRTIES' THE SUN FLARES UP, GETTING HOTTER WITH FRUSTRATION.

DURING LATER LIFE IT BECOMES RED-FACED, SWELLING WITH POMPOUS FURY.

IN OLD AGE IT SHRINKS, COOLS AND TURNS WHITE.

FINALLY, THE SUN BECOMES DARK, DEAD AND COLD FOR ALL ETERNITY.

167

Environmental Degradation

It's not just the upper atmosphere we're screwing up. We're making a mess of things down here as well. And some scientists believe that a cumulative disaster could catch us by surprise.

We've got used to the mantra of ecologists by now. We do a bit of recycling, pity the polar bears and put some change in the WWF cup. When we sometimes buy a cheeseburger meal deal and get no fewer than 17 articles of paper and plastic packaging with it, we furtively dump it as soon as possible. We never see the giant panda or the tiger, and the only cod we come across is covered in breadcrumbs on a plastic tray.

HERE ARE SOME PRACTICAL SUGGESTIONS

- RE-USE MY PLASTIC BAGS
- TAKE AN ASPRIN EVERY DAY
- DRINK LOW-FAT MILK
- WRITE TO MY MP ABOUT: NUCLEAR POWER/ WIND POWER/COAL POWER *
  - * DELETE 1 OR ALL
- STOP BUYING CHEAP THINGS MADE BY CHILDREN
- SHOP LOCAL INSTEAD OF DRIVING TO THE SUPERMARKET
- GET IMMUNISED
- EAT MORE NUTS AND BLUEBERRIES
- EAT CHOCOLATE
- GET RID OF MY TV
- THROW AWAY KNICKERS AND TIGHTS MADE FROM FOSSIL FUELS
- KILL MYSELF AND REDUCE THE POPULATION
- STOP USING A CAR AND WALK EVERYWHERE IN BARE FEET
- STOP WASHING, USING MAKE-UP AND PERFUME AND GO ABOUT NAKED
- RENOUNCE MONEY
- USE MORE SUN-BLOCK
- STOP BUYING NEW TECHNOLOGY EVERY FEW MONTHS
- GET AN ALLOTMENT
- STOP FLYING IN PLANES
- BECOME VEGETARIAN

CONFUSED?

LET **FATE** CHOOSE FOR YOU. SIMPLY CLOSE YOUR EYES, PLUNK YOUR FINGER ON THIS PAGE AND ACT ACCORDINGLY...

Naw...

One person won't make a difference...

More fries, please.

a) Coral Reef Destruction

Coral reefs are beautiful. They draw tourists by the millions and provide income for countries with not much else to offer sightseers. They are a model of biodiversity, with countless species of fish and other sea creatures on which the economies of small fishing communities depend. Called the 'rainforests of the sea', they are a rich source of medicines for such maladies as heart disease, leukaemia and ulcers. They have been around for millions of years.

And we're killing them off.

Oil spills, waste dumping and other by-products of human activity are causing their destruction, as does acidification of the sea. Recently we have learned that oestrogen-like compounds entering the environment are disrupting the reproductive lives of the small marine polyps that form the reefs (see pages 146–4).

We have already lost 10% of the world's coral reefs. In the Philippines, the number is closer to 70%.

Sad, but so what?

Some 25% of the world's fish live near the reefs. In marginal communities that depend upon them, this means famine. Such a loss in numbers would add to the already stressed populations of food fish, and bring the global food crisis one step nearer.

Coral reefs protect coasts from erosion and deterioration

through storm surges. Many places that are now favourite holiday spots would disappear or become useless. This would create more migration, more economic stress and more conflict.

THE LIFE CYCLE OF CORAL

i ~ MALE CORAL — FEMALE CORAL

ii ~ POLLUTION CAUSES MALE CORAL TO TURN FEMALE

iii ~ GAY CORAL PERFECTLY HAPPY BUT NO LONGER PRODUCING BABY CORAL

iv ~ NO CORAL

Even if you live in a landlocked country, never travel and don't eat fish and chips, you're helping to wipe out this natural treasure every day. So don't point the finger at the snorkellers.

We're all to blame.

b) Vanishing Fish Stocks

Coral reefs? Big deal. There are plenty more fish in the sea.

Or are there?

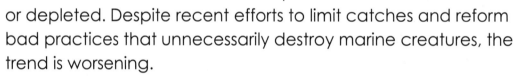

Signs are that we're emptying the seas of fish. According to marine biologists, we have enough fishing capacity to serve four planets the size of Earth. Yet more than 25% of fish stocks are either overexploited or depleted. Despite recent efforts to limit catches and reform bad practices that unnecessarily destroy marine creatures, the trend is worsening.

Some species are so rare that the price has shot up to astronomical levels. A few years ago, a very large bluefin tuna sold at a Tokyo market for £250,000. This is a shade higher than what you might expect to pay in your local chippy, but it points to the fact that highly desirable fish are, quite simply, running out. Even your favourite, *Gadus morhua*, probably known to you as North Atlantic cod, is at critical levels. Remember when fish and chips was a cheap meal?

But the problem affects more than our wallets. Biologists warn that overfishing and species depletion is causing ecological changes to the oceans, which have a fragile balance to maintain in such things as oxygen and sea temperatures.

Sad about the fish, but at least we've saved the whales and dolphins. Haven't we?

More than 20,000 dolphins are killed each year off the coast of Japan. As for whales, pressure by Japan, Iceland and other countries continues on the international community to ease restrictions. 'Scientific research' allowances give countries the right to kill up to 1,000 each year.

Bad news for Flipper. Bad news for us, too.

COMMIT THESE FISH TO MEMORY
YOU WON'T GET TO SEE THEM AGAIN

COD & CHIPS

HAKE & CHIPS

SALMON FISHCAKES

PLAICE & CHIPS

TURBOT & MASH

RED SNAPPER & NEW POTATOES

KIPPERS & BREAD & BUTTER

FISH FINGERS & BEANS

FISH-IN-A-BAG & FROZEN PEAS

AS GOOD AS NEW!

IN THE FUTURE CLEVER HUMANS USING INFLATABLE FISH WILL BRING THE OCEANS BACK TO LIFE

NOT TO SCALE

A FLOCK OF HELIUM-FILLED FLYING FISH →

Oops.

POP!

INFLATABLE FISH CAN ROAM FOR YEARS, THANKS TO SMALL ELECTRIC MOTORS

A SHOAL OF BATTERY-POWERED MULLET

DEAD CORAL

CRABBING TRAPS. FISHERMEN CATCH THE CRABS, WIND THEM UP, THEN RETURN THEM TO THE DEPTHS

CLOCKWORK CRABS

158

c) Tropical Deforestation

Anyone for a spot of tree-cutting?

Near the equator, all around the Earth are the areas of greatest biological diversity and productivity. The rainforests of places like Brazil are home to the largest numbers of species known to the planet. We are only beginning to scratch the surface of identifying them. Biologists believe that they probably contain cures for cancer and other diseases, in addition to their many other life-giving properties. They represent the deep end of the earthly gene pool. They help regulate the oxygen levels in our atmosphere, and, according to research by NASA, could make a vital difference in helping to sustain the Earth in the event of a catastrophic 'extinction event'.

These forests are being cut down at an astonishing rate. If you look at time-lapse satellite photos of the last few years you can see them disappearing like melting snow.

So who's cutting them down? You are. That is, unless you never

use latex, cork, fruit, nuts, timber, fibres, spices, natural oils and resins or medicines. Not only that, when you buy beef products or grains grown in recently cleared areas of the forests, you might as well have gone out for a day's work with a chainsaw.

The people who do the deforestation are not ignorant or heedless. Education programmes have been around for years that try to alert the mainly poor exploiters of the forests about the need for sustainability. People need income, because they want to buy some of the things we take for granted. It always just happens one tree at a time.

Something to think about in the cancer ward or when the air gets too thin to breathe. Maybe any one of the problems of deforestation and ocean degradation mentioned above won't be enough to kill us off. But maybe a combination of overexploited resources and ignored scientific warnings will. There are lots of other things we haven't mentioned, all of which add up rapidly.

But you know what they are, don't you?

Ozone-layer Depletion

Did you ever wonder why Australian cricketers still wear that funny white cream on their faces? Wasn't that all about holes in the ozone layer, and haven't we solved that by now?

The white cream is a sunblock. They still wear it because the most optimistic forecast for the restoration of the ozone layer to 1980 levels is 2068. Meanwhile, we are at risk from melanoma, cataracts and crop failure.

The Montreal Protocol of 1989 banned the manufacture and use of CFCs, which were commonly used as propellants in spray cans and as a gas for refrigeration. It has made a remarkable impact on the amounts of new fluorocarbons found in the upper atmosphere, scientists tell us.

But it's still up there.

No one agrees about the long-term effects the polar 'ozone holes' will have on Earth life. Where the layer has been all or nearly all depleted, there have been rises in some dread diseases like basal and squamous cell carcinomas.

Oddly, it has been proposed that a depletion in the ozone layer could cause cooling in the stratosphere. By making the Earth cooler, this might possibly offset the rate of global warming. But at the same time, the very gases that wipe out the ozone are 'greenhouse gases', so it could go either way.

Keep your sunscreen handy. We'll just have to wait and see.

153

Species Extinction

The passenger pigeon, the stegosaurus and the dodo are all kaput. Who's next?

The problem of species extinction isn't a new one. The dinosaurs vanished 65 million years ago after being around for 150 million years. Theories range from an asteroid impact in the Caribbean Sea to an unknown contagious disease. Species disappear when their environmental conditions change, slowly or drastically. This process has always been with us.

But now it's happening faster, and to a lot more animals and plants than we can keep track of. Our grandchildren won't be able to see white rhinos on a vacation safari. Some of those interesting vines that tangle the rainforests might be gone before we ever clock them.

Sad news, but . . . so what?

Ecology is a fledgling science, but we already know how complex it is. Taking just the rain forests, we know that more than 50,000 plant and animal species become extinct every year following deforestation.

Of these, only about 1% have ever been studied. Some scientists believe that the cures for many illnesses, including cancer, may be locked up in the lost flora. Already, 25% of our medicines are based on rainforest plants.

Plants make oxygen. People make CO_2. Assuming that

carbon dioxide is the major culprit in global warming, losing plants means raising temperatures.

Over-cultivation of food crops takes us further and further from the original rootstock of plants. When a new disease strikes, such as that affecting the banana, we may have lost the basic genetic material that might save the species.

Every time an insect species disappears, such as the honey-bee, it takes along with it part of the vital function of pollination of our food and fibre crops.

We may be on a countdown to our own extinction without knowing it. If a tree falls in the forest and there's no one around to hear it, does it make a sound?

Yes. Tick-tock.

Yes, We Have No Bananas

Take the humble banana.

BANANA GRAPH

SHOWING HOW MUCH BANANAS WILL BE MISSED

- - - - LOTS

- - - - A BIT

- - NOT AT ALL

I NEVER - - LIKED THEM ANYWAY

- - I'M ALLERGIC

- - - GOOD RIDDENCE

- YUK!

Scientists fear that this much-loved breakfast fruit is on its way out, after 15,000 years of human cultivation. Because it has been so intensively grown, it lacks the genetic diversity essential to fight off opportunistic bacterial and fungal infestations.

There has already been one banana apocalypse, when the species of the fruit known as Gros Michel (Big Mike) was wiped out by a fungus related to Dutch elm disease. Big Mike was said to be sweeter and more flavourful than the Cavendish variety we eat nowadays. Now the Panama fungus threatens all remaining versions of the fruit.

The real possibility of Doom is only implied by the banana plague. How many of our over-cultivated and genetically altered crops could fall prey to the same fate? In our successful domination of nature, have we left our genetic flanks fatally exposed?

INTRODUCING THE *artificial* BANANA!

MADE FROM SOYA BEANS AND SQUASHED INTO A BANANA SHAPE, IT IS DYED YELLOW AND TURNS BLACK JUST LIKE THE REAL THING!

fig a ~

fig b ~

NB - CAN NO LONGER BE CALLED A FRUIT

Bloody things! I thought they were extinct!

Honeybees

No more bee stings? No more weird guys with bee beards? No more honey on our pancakes?

That's the possible future, according to scientists. The humble honeybee is on its way out.

CLICK
WHIRRR
CLICK

This is due to 'colony collapse disorder', when bee colonies suddenly lose critical mass in population and spiral towards death. The major culprits are believed to be pesticides and a newly identified viral infection. This organism thrives in the guts of overwintering bees and quickly spreads throughout the hive. More than a third of the North American bee population is likely to disappear over the next year.

And now there's even worse news: you might be killing off bees every time you use your mobile phone.

CLICK
CLICK
CLICK
CLICK...

A recent study at Panjab University in India showed that fixing mobile phones to a hive for two 15-minute periods each day for three months caused bees to stop producing honey, reduced the queen's egg production by half and brought about a drastic reduction in bee numbers. Because bees may rely on magnetic fields for direction, flooding the environment with cellphone signals may make them unable to find their way back to the hive.

Sad. But can't we live without honey on our pancakes?

Think again. The problem isn't just with the buzzing insects: 90% of food crops rely upon insect pollination, and bees are by far the most effective. If bees were to become extinct, the effect on world food supplies would be catastrophic, and worsen the already declining ability of humans to feed themselves. Subsistence farmers could find themselves plunged into famine in a

WHIRRRRR...

short period of time, and all of us would feel it.

CHUG
CHUG
CHUG
CHUG

Fewer bees means fewer plants means fewer bees means...

Fewer of us.

NO BEES? NO PROBLEM!

SCIENTISTS WILL REPLACE ALL THE REAL BEES WITH TINY ROBOT VERSIONS. AS WELL AS POLLINATING FLOWERS, THE ARTIFICIAL BEES WILL BE ABLE TO COLLECT POLLEN, MAKE HONEY, PACK IT IN JARS, STICK ON LABELS AND DELIVER IT TO THE SHOPS.

THEIR STINGS WILL BE INTENSELY PLEASURABLE.

Gender Erosion

Is every creature on Earth becoming female?

Scientists think so. Lately they have discovered alarming levels of oestrogen in our rivers and lakes. Oestrogen is the cocktail of hormones that make half of the human race female. Everybody has some of it – even men.

Oestrogen leaks into the environment through sewage treatment and the coating of aluminium tins. Like many chemical by-products of industry, these substances don't just go away.

Recent studies have identified male fish with female sex organs and anatomically deformed otters, not to mention a dramatic shrinkage of penis size in Florida alligators.

DOOM SCENARIO:
MALE EVOLUTION

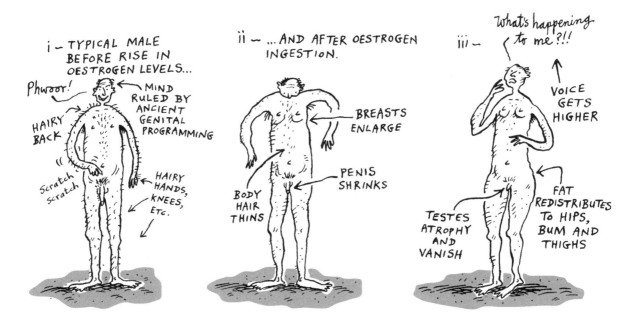

Many scientists believe that human fertility is decreasing through the ingestion of oestrogen from public water supplies.

Marine biologists worry that high levels of oestrogen will wreck the sex lives of coral reefs, resulting in a shortfall of the world's fish crop of at least a quarter.

No one is sure what to do, but one proposal for removing oestrogen from water supplies has come from the University of Ulster, which has '...discovered that if you shine an ultraviolet light on titanium dioxide, the titanium becomes activated, and capable of converting the oestrogen to CO_2 – the harmless everyday gas that puts the bubbles in your fizzy pop.'

Carbon dioxide or oestrogen: pick your poison.

Global Food Crisis

We thought he was banished forever, but we were wrong. One of the original Four Horsemen of the Apocalypse seems not to have gone away, after all.

HUNGRY!

Waaaa...

Famine.

Our experience with starvation on a large scale has mostly been limited to those terrible television images of Africans during droughts. Emaciated babies, grieving mothers huddled in makeshift shelters, the mass graves. It made us feel so bad that we gave a record amount of money for emergency relief. Pop stars wrote songs and held concerts. Governments made promises. We switched channels.

But the spectre of mass starvation is back. The world is facing fast-approaching scarcities of just about everything necessary to produce enough food for everyone. The lack of fresh water, arable land, nutrients, oil and fats, technology, skills, fish stocks and reliable climates is leading to a famine of hitherto unknown magnitude. And it's projected for sometime this century.

How could this happen?

International organisations monitoring world food supplies warn that a number of interlocking phenomena have created a tangle that we may not be able to escape from. In

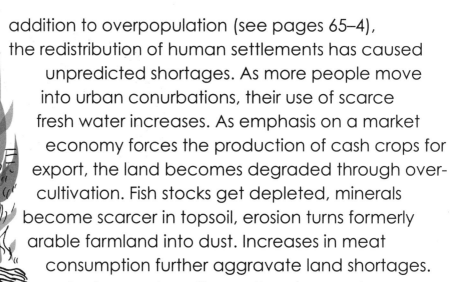

addition to overpopulation (see pages 65–4), the redistribution of human settlements has caused unpredicted shortages. As more people move into urban conurbations, their use of scarce fresh water increases. As emphasis on a market economy forces the production of cash crops for export, the land becomes degraded through over-cultivation. Fish stocks get depleted, minerals become scarcer in topsoil, erosion turns formerly arable farmland into dust. Increases in meat consumption further aggravate land shortages. And on and on. The pattern is complex, and may seem unbreakable without massive changes in the way we live.

Starvation is not the only way famine turns into Doom. When food gets scarce, prices rise. When high-quality, nutritious food becomes too expensive, people have less of it, become sick, less capable and subject to disease. Mass migration from places of little food to richer sites creates economic and political strife. Ultimately, famine leads to another of the Four Horsemen.

War.

FAMINE, WAR AND THE OTHER 27 HORSEMEN OF THE APOCALYPSE

Fossil-fuel Depletion

Oil and gas won't last forever.

That's not news, because we've been hearing it for almost all our lives. If we think about it, we probably just picture windmills humming in some remote future, or hydrogen-fuelled limousines zipping healthily down the motorways. But some scientists are warning us that the tipping point for an energy crisis is nearer than we think.

No one knows exactly when the last drop of oil will be pumped out of the ground. Estimates vary from ten to 65 years. In most scenarios, oil, gas and coal gradually run out, making it cheaper to switch to wind, solar and tidal sources. Helpful industries will find ways to make the transition seamless. We won't even have to give up trips to Machu Picchu and weekends in Las Vegas.

But some scientists warn that we're heading for a 'cliff event'.

This prediction envisions a few sharp shocks as extreme shortages and blackouts multiply and nations begin a policy of energy hoarding with consequent political and military results.

A CLIFF EVENT

Oops...

SOME THINGS WE WON'T HAVE WHEN FOSSIL FUELS RUN OUT:

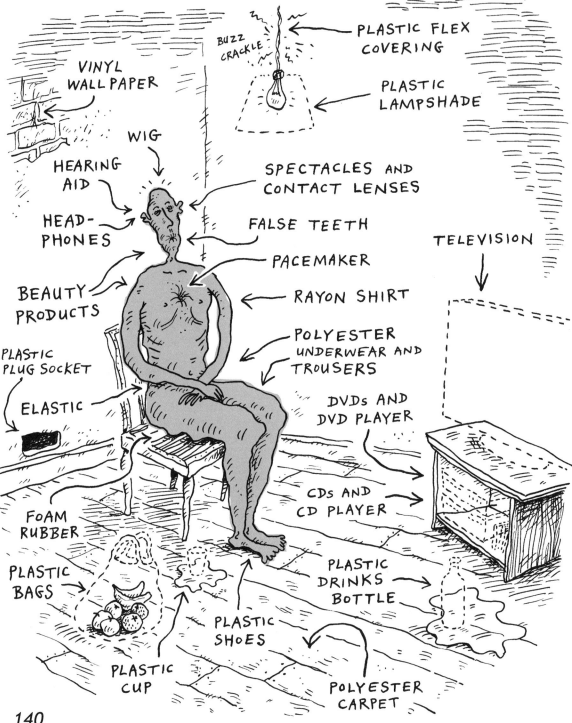

140

We wouldn't have to wait for absolute depletion because disruption in supply would bring on a crisis. The result would be dramatic, not gradual.

Shortages would lead to a scenario that imitates what has happened in famines. Prices would shoot up. The poorest communities would suddenly go from having little energy to having none at all. Widespread chaos would affect the political sphere.

With the loss of inexpensive petroleum products, we would lose more than just fuel for heating and transport. More than 70,000 products we use daily would either disappear or become prohibitively expensive. Things like computer components, mobile phones, eyeglass lenses, common medicines and replacement heart valves would be unaffordable.

Some historians speculate that the entire story of modern civilisation is merely a blip on the long line of pre-industrial existence. The discovery of oil made us leap forward technologically, and its disappearance may make us fall back.

Stone axes to satellites, then back to stone axes.

139

137

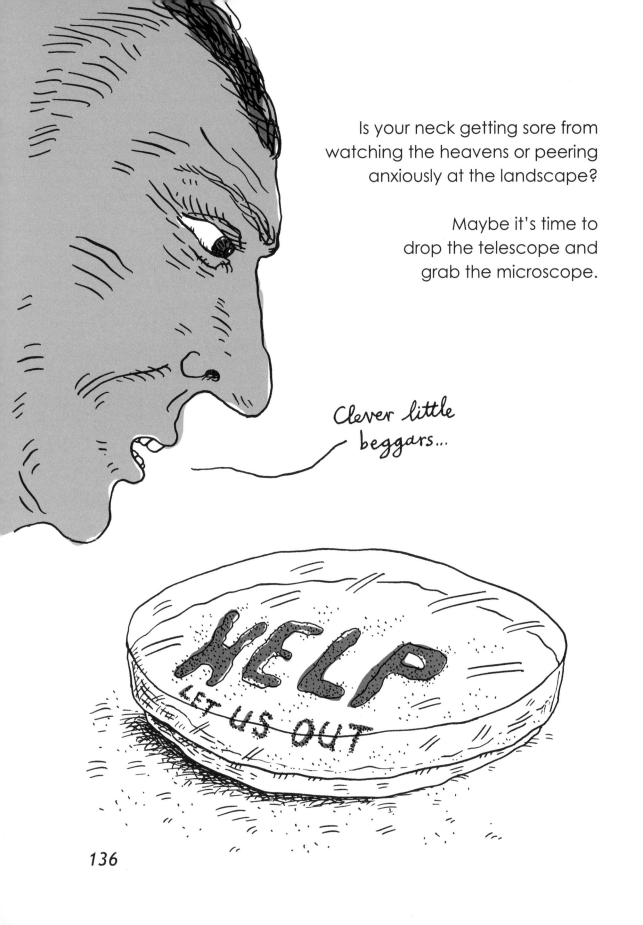

Microbial War

While we were worried about the superweapons being developed by our enemies in other countries, a much more ancient enemy was developing a sneak attack that is capable of killing people by the million.

Bacteria.  1000s OF BACTERIA CAN FIT ON THE HEAD OF A PIN

Ever since Alexander Fleming discovered penicillin by accident one day in 1928, we have relaxed our fear of these tiny organisms. Diseases that used to kill us were banished with a single jab. Dread sexually transmitted maladies became a thing of the past. It seemed that we had found a magic bullet that would protect us from all those things that plagued our ancestors.

It is true that we heard that strains of bacteria were evolving in ways that foiled treatment with antibiotics, but the clever folk in white lab coats made sure we were ahead of the game by developing new and stronger drugs.

Until now.

When antibiotics were first used, bacteria were hit by threats a million times more potent than anything they had faced before. It should have been game over. But bacteria aren't pushovers. Their response was to evolve a million times faster.

We hit back with newer and stronger formulae. They responded with even trickier moves. In the last 80 years, there has been a see-saw battle going on in arenas too small to see.

As long as we kept ahead of them, we could avoid the possibility of new infections for which we have no inbuilt defences. But that's all over now.

PLACE YOUR
FINGERTIP
ON THIS SPOT ➝ ●

NOW REMOVE IT

YOU HAVE JUST DEPOSITED
A FEW <u>MILLION</u> BACTERIA

NEXT, LICK YOUR FINGERTIP AND
RUB IT ON THE PAGE

YOU HAVE PROBABLY NOW DEPOSITED
CLOSE TO A <u>BILLION</u>*

BETTER BURN THIS BOOK AND BUY
A FRESH, CLEAN COPY. DON'T FORGET
TO READ IT WEARING RUBBER GLOVES

According to an article by Catherine Paddock in *Medical News Today*, the previous rate of new antibiotic products was about 15 per decade. The last ten years have seen only six. The reason is that pharmaceutical companies are reluctant to invest in a drug that will only be saleable for ten years. Meanwhile, the bacteria are getting stronger, mutating happily, gaining ground (see pages 130–29).

It's the longest war humans have ever fought. And the bad guys are winning.

* These figures are disputed by Professor Alan McCarthy, department of microbiology, Liverpool University, who considers them grossly inflated.

133

Flu Pandemic

Let's be honest: we're all waiting for the next pandemic.

True, we've had near brushes with swine flu, avian flu and SARS. And not nearly as many people got sick and died as we feared. Scientists are beetling away in labs, tracking the mutations in diseases that begin in ducks and pigs. Provided that they keep on the job, we should be OK, right?

Think again.

Out there in places we've never heard of, viruses are plying their trade of inhabiting warm-blooded hosts. Their lab is the whole muddy world, and ours is just a few clean white buildings. They change and reproduce with such speed that they are becoming impossible to predict or control.

The Spanish flu pandemic of 1918 was so bad that it killed somewhere between 40 and 50 million people, more than the Great War it so closely followed. In the USA alone, 28% of the population was infected and the death rate was so high that life expectancy estimates were down-rated by ten years. Everyone was fearful. A jump-rope song of the period went like this:

I had a little bird,
Its name was Enza.
I opened the window,
And in-flu-enza.

It was formerly believed that pandemic flu followed the traditional pattern by attacking the weakest members of the population. But strains like the H1N1 variety can occur at any age. Ominously, the virus seems most deadly in young adults, not in the traditional at-risk categories of infancy and the elderly.

YOU CAN GET A FATAL DISEASE LEADING TO DEATH ALMOST ANYWHERE ON, OR IN, YOUR BODY.

THIS DIAGRAM SHOWS SOME PLACES TO CHECK REGULARLY.

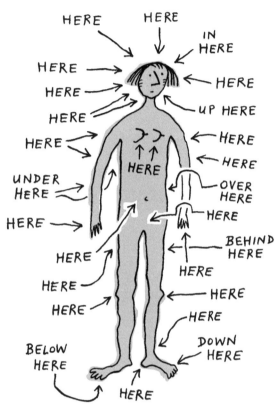

Because of the speed and stealth of pandemic contagion, the fear is that a new strain of something like H1N1 will strike before there is any time to prepare, decimating an entire generation, striking those most vital to keeping things running, like hospitals. And ambulances. And flu research labs.

What can we do?

Wash your hands. And don't open the window.

Superbugs

Are miracle drugs past their sell-by date? Could we be returning to a situation like that before the 20th century when we were dropping like flies from simple diseases we have since almost written off? It appears so. A new superbug is threatening to end the life-saving ability of antibiotics – all antibiotics.

And it's all down to promiscuous bacteria.

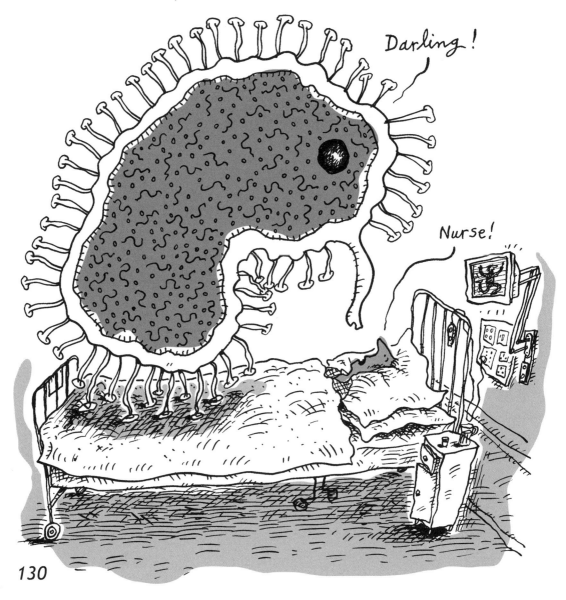

NDM-1 was first seen in India in 2008. It has the ability to produce an enzyme that can make bacteria such as E-coli immune to carbapenems, broad-spectrum antibiotics distantly related to penicillin.

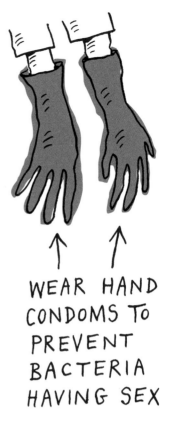

WEAR HAND CONDOMS TO PREVENT BACTERIA HAVING SEX

According to Hugh Pennington, Emeritus Professor of Bacteriology at the University of Aberdeen, bacteria, though they don't need sex to reproduce, have it anyway. By deliberately jumping on to each other like randy teenagers, they spread the enzyme, making even simple germs able to laugh at drug treatment.

In an age of 'medical tourism', when patients might spend time in different hospitals on separate continents, the bug travels easily. It has recently appeared in NHS wards in rapidly increasing numbers.

At present, the only defence on offer is a renewed appeal for handwashing and hospital sanitation. But success in this area is notoriously difficult to achieve. In places like Scandinavia and Holland, patients transferred from British hospitals are routinely assumed to carry the MRSA bacterium.

As Dr Pennington said in an article in the *Daily Telegraph*, hoping for new antibiotics to combat the NDM-1 and other micro-villains remains just that.

Hope.

Ebola (Haemorrhagic Fever)

There are just a few diseases that make epidemiologists shudder. One of these is Ebola.

This virus has been found in West and Central Africa, where it has killed a few hundred people in several outbreaks. It is zoonotic (animal-borne), and is often found in primates. It causes high fever and a generalised infection of body organs, which begin to bleed. Recovery rates are low, and anything up to 88% of infected people die from it, usually horribly, in a few weeks.

Scientists believe it is transmitted by the body fluids of an infected animal or person. In some of the largest known epidemics in places like the Republic of the Congo, most victims were either close family or health care workers, who caught it from patients.

THE ETIQUETTE OF SAFE SNEEZING

fig i ~ Ah ah ah...

fig ii ~ CHOO!

In laboratory conditions, doctors have found the spores of the virus in droplets in breath. Contagion is not known to have followed as a result of breathing in aerosol particles. But viruses

128

are clever, and have the ability to mutate rapidly.

So far, major outbreaks of the virus have been avoided. Precautions such as surgical gloves and face masks have limited its spread. As with other diseases, such as retroviral ones like HIV AIDS, it is believed you probably can't get it unless you eat dead chimpanzees or come into contact with someone else's bodily secretions.

Moral: Unsafe sex might get a lot unsafer.

125

Super Volcano

Just a few miles away from us there's a giant ball of burning rock the size of the Earth. This rock is so hot that it's in liquid form, capable of instantly incinerating everything it touches.

You don't need a telescope to find it. It's just under our feet.

Volcanoes erupt when the pressure caused by massive temperatures forces an aperture in the Earth's crust. As in the Icelandic eruption of 2010, clouds of smoke and dust stream into the atmosphere. This dust can cause disruption to travel and cooling of nearby regions as it blocks sunlight. But these are the small fry of eruptions. There are a few which can alter history and even end it.

Super volcanoes.

This name is given to a class of eruptions that we know about only from geological evidence. We've never witnessed one, because we probably wouldn't still be around if we had. We might have shared the fate of the Neanderthals, who some scientists believe were finished off by the eruption of a south Italian volcano 40,000 years ago.

Take Yellowstone.

This site in Wyoming is the largest super volcano known. If it erupts, some of the effects would be the complete devastation of an area the size of Europe, a coating of ash ranging from six inches to hundreds of feet over thousands of miles, a 'winter' caused by clouds of dust and ash that lasts several years, the widespread failure of food crops, probable species extinction and the lowering of global temperatures by up to 20 degrees.

In some ways, volcanoes are predictable. The intervals between eruptions have been noted by geologists and backed up by palaeontologists. Yellowstone, for example, has a schedule of eruption activity every 600,000 years or so. The last time it blew up was about 640,000 years ago. Worryingly, geologists have confirmed a recent bulging of the terrain at the site of the volcano, or caldera. This could mean the magma is starting to act.

Of course, it is 40,000 years overdue.

A VOLCANIC EXPERIMENT TO TRY AT HOME

i ~ FILL A BUCKET WITH ASH AND DUST FROM THE VACUUM CLEANER.

ii ~ PRETEND YOU'RE AN EVIL MASTERMIND AND LAUNCH YOUR 'MISSILE' TOWARDS THE SITTING-ROOM CEILING.

Whee!

iii ~ IMAGINE THE SITTING ROOM IS THE WORLD. IMPRESSIVE, HUH?

iv ~ EXPERIMENT OVER. TIME TO GO WATCH TV.

I'm going to KILL you, you... you...

Mega-tsunami

Earthquakes cause tidal waves. So no earthquake, no tsunami, right?

Wrong, say the scientists.

There's a large chunk of rock teetering on the edge of the Canary Islands that could cause a mega-tsunami of sufficient size to devastate the eastern seaboard of the United States. This is the entire western slope of Cumbre Vieja on the island of La Palma, the site of volcanoes that stretch back to the creation of the island chain itself.

Geologists say that, following an eruption in 1949, a deformity in the rock structure has opened a crack behind a piece of mountain measuring up to 500 cubic kilometres. If you spread that mass out one yard deep, you come up with an area three times the size of Washington, DC. If it falls all at once, it will make a splash like no other in recorded history.

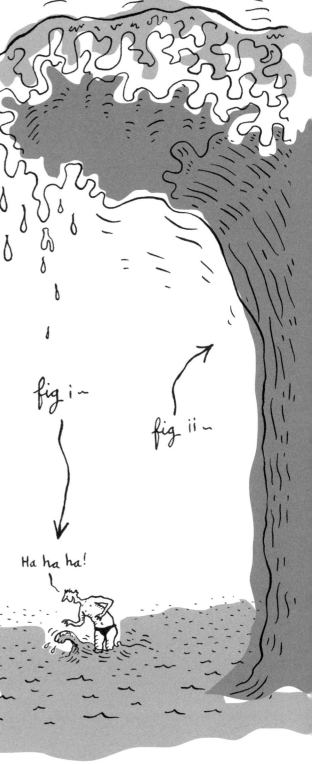

fig i ~

fig ii ~

Ha ha ha!

The worst-case scenario, according to the Benfield Hazard Research Centre at University College, London, is a wall of water the height of a 17-storey building that would cross the Atlantic at the speed of a jumbo jet in full flight.

New York City would be entirely flattened, as would the whole of the most populous area of the US. Large sections of the Caribbean islands would be under water, and some projections say the backwash would severely affect Ireland, France and the western UK.

More recent studies have proposed that this danger has been overstated because the landslide might occur in more gradual stages, with less devastating results. But Ben McGuire, the Benfield director, points to similar events that have occurred within geological history. One example is unexplained large boulders that have been found in the Bahamas 20 metres above sea level, almost certainly carried there by giant waves. On the Canary Island of El Hierro, an escarpment left behind by a previous event contains melted rock, evidence of a dramatic and sudden slippage.

But it's not just the next eruption of Cumbre Vieja which has scientists worried.

The crack in the mountain is gradually being filled with rain-water, which further erodes its stability. When the crack fills up entirely, there will be very little holding the land mass in place.

Recently, rainfall in the Canaries has been at record highs.

Clathrate Gun Hypothesis

Maybe global warming is a gradual process.
Maybe we will have time to adjust and
take measures to keep the Earth habitable.

And maybe we won't.

Trapped beneath the permafrost in the Arctic are huge
deposits of a gas called methane clathrate. As long as the
polar regions stay comfortably frozen, this
gas stays out of the atmosphere. In the
event of melting permafrost, however,
this gas could explode into the
atmosphere with such speed that it has
been called a 'methane gun'.

Methane is a greenhouse gas 60 times more
powerful than carbon dioxide. A sudden release of any of the
known deposits would trigger a catastrophic heating of the
Earth. This may have taken place during the
Permo–Triassic extinction event, when
the temperature of the globe was
raised by six degrees. If it happened
again, extinction of most earthly life
would almost certainly follow.

Including us.

Most layers of methane clathrate are too deep to surface
easily. But in the Siberian Arctic, the deposits are shallowly
submerged, with just a layer of permafrost on top. If the

climate keeps on heating up, the margins grow thinner and thinner. Any sudden boost in the rate of warming could tip the scales and bring about what has been called 'runaway global warming'.

It would be sad to see the polar bears losing their habitat if the ice keeps melting. Even worse if the Gulf Stream lost its power to keep us warm. But those aren't the only problems.

If the permafrost disappears, so do we.

SEARCHING FOR SURVIVAL SOLUTIONS, №1:

Am I getting warm?

I think we all are.

MIKE HAS CONVERTED HIS FRIDGE INTO A HOME

Radon

Just beneath your floor there's a severe threat to your survival. This silent killer is responsible for more than 21,000 deaths per year in the United States. Radon 222. Some areas are more affected, others less so, but no one is totally safe from it without drastic measures being taken to protect their homes.

HOW TO DETECT RADON GAS IN YOUR CELLAR

SNIFF SNIFF

Radon gas is the result of the decay of uranium, which is found in most soils. It is particularly prevalent in mines, but appears in nearly all house basements and under flooring slabs. It has been known about since at least the 16th century, when it was noticed that miners were acquiring a mysterious 'wasting disease', but it wasn't until the 1980s that scientists first began to measure its effects on human health. It is now considered the second largest cause of lung cancer.

Around that time people began worrying about what they were inhaling at home. A flock of new preventative techniques surfaced, such as putting ventilation systems beneath basement floors and radiation sheathing under concrete slabs. New construction regulations appeared in the US, and as recently as 2010, Britain published new safe limits. Test kits are available for home testing, but these have not been widely taken up.

TRYING TO CATCH
RADON AS IT RISES

After the radon mini-panic in the 1980s, it seems we have become used to the idea that even the air we breathe holds dire threats to our survival. Just like we did with the flu pandemics that fizzled out.

Ho-hum. Sssssssss...

LETTING THE
RADON ESCAPE
HARMLESSLY

CARBON
FOOTPRINTS

113

Climate Change

We've got big problems with the climate.

You and I, in our heedless consumption of resources and the consequential dumping of carbon atoms into the atmosphere, may have brought about a disastrous future – global warming.

Scientists predict that the climate will heat up by between one and 3.5 degrees Celsius during this century. If that doesn't sound like a lot, we are told that the lowering of temperatures by just half a degree following a volcanic eruption in 1816 caused crop failures all over the world. There's not a lot of margin in our ecosystem.

THE WORLD'S GOING TO HELL ANYWAY, SO WHY NOT ENJOY FAN HEATER IN-A-CAN™

Spray yourself with aerosol heat WHENEVER and WHEREVER you need it.

Cool! Er, hot.

According to the International Panel on Climate Change, we can expect sea level rises that put more than 100 million people at risk of tidal flooding and lost land. Several Pacific nations will completely disappear. Evaporation rates will rise too, causing deserts to eat away existing farmland. Heat stress will kill many people, as the hot summer of 2003 did to more than 14,000 in France.

Many species will become extinct in even moderate warming.

WHY NOT PLOT CLIMATE CHANGE AS IT HAPPENS?

SIMPLY COLOUR IN THE THERMOMETER AS STATISTICS ARE RELEASED

Brilliant! I can't wait for the temperature to go up!

One scientist has said that in order to survive, species will have to migrate away from the Equator at the rate of nine metres a day.

Famine from loss of arable land and shrinking of fresh water supplies may strike even the lush farmlands of temperate zones. We can expect massive storms, called 'hypercanes', that make Hurricane Katrina look like a summer rain shower. And it's all our fault.

Unless it isn't.

Sceptics abound. The unwillingness to believe that humans are responsible for anything as big as the weather has created a new category of problem people: climate-change deniers.

The best of these difficult types stop short of denying that temperatures are gradually rising. They point to such evidence as the recent discovery of the remains of huge

TOAST!
HELP!
AAARGH...
YOU CAN BOIL WATER
I SEE YOU ALREADY HAVE
IT'S HOT ENOUGH TO COOK AN EGG
UNBEARABLE
OOPS. THE AIR CON BROKE DOWN
THANK GOD FOR AIR CON
BLIMEY...
PHEW! IT'S HOT
BETTER SIT IN THE SHADE
WE CAN PUT THE CAR ROOF DOWN
LOVELY WEATHER FOR A PICNIC
VERY NICE
OOH, YES...
PLEASANT
BEARABLE
CHILLY (NOT 'CHILLI')
BRRR!
JOLLY COLD
FREEZING!

111

trees in Antarctica to show that the climate is always changing. They invoke solar activity and other natural agents as the source of change in the weather.

A more tenacious group of deniers say that the climate isn't changing at all. They point to some unfortunate recent claims of data fiddling by academics. This empowers them to scoff at the data that hasn't been fudged. Following the lead of some reckless US politicians, their rallying cry has become 'Drill, baby, drill!'

But are they the ones who are fiddling, as the world burns?

A TERRIFYING DOOM SCENARIO!

fig 1 —
I'm BoRED of hearing about climate change...
YAWN...

I don't believe it's really happening.

fig 2 —
Let's go shopping in my new 4 × 4.

CARBON FOOTPRINTS

A DIAGRAM EXPLAINING

OVERCONSUMPTION & CLIMATE CHANGE

GREENHOUSE GASES

GAS GAS GAS GAS GAS GAS GAS GAS GAS GAS GAS GAS GAS GAS

TRAVELLING

PRODUCING

GENERATING

EATING

FLOWERS

TRANSPORTING

Cheap CLOTHES

SUPER-SUPERMARKET

CONSUMING

DELIVERING

HANDBAGS & SHOES

I... want...   mine!

Need...

DESIRING   Need

AFRICA

a) Vector-borne Diseases

Warmer temperatures don't sound all that bad, you say. Maybe we won't get as many colds and cases of flu.

Maybe we'll get malaria instead.

The World Health Organisation has warned that unchecked warming in northern latitudes could bring back diseases we haven't had to deal with in centuries. Things like malaria, encephalitis and dengue fever. Carried by insects, these ailments already account for more than three-quarters of a million deaths per year, many more than from HIV AIDS.

A warmer climate in the north means longer summers, a wetter atmosphere, and more damp breeding places for mosquitoes and other sources of 'vector-borne' diseases.

The mild increase in temperature we have already experienced–about 0.8 degrees Celsius–has made Azerbaijan, Tajikistan and Turkey danger areas for malaria. Predictions are that the carriers will gradually spread west and north into the temperate zone.

At present, 90% of malaria cases occur in sub-Saharan Africa. The death toll is very high, but probably less than it might be because of gradually acquired resistance to the disease through selection. In northern Europe, we have rarely had to become resistant, so the death toll would probably be much higher.

To add to the threat, ticks and sandflies, carriers of such illnesses as Lyme disease and visceral leishmaniasis, would also find the new, warmer climate agreeable.

So far, no measures beyond computer projections have been taken.

TO COMBAT CLIMATE CHANGE, SIMPLY START USING SOME OF THE EXCITING **NEW** ECO-PRODUCTS BELOW...

REPLACE YOUR TUMBLE DRYER WITH THIS INNOVATIVE SOLAR AND WIND POWERED DEVICE:

AND HOW ABOUT TRADING IN YOUR CENTRAL HEATING FOR ONE OF THESE CLEVER ITEMS?

b) Killer Bees

Mosquitoes aren't the only flying peril to move north with the warming climate. A slip-up by a replacement beekeeper in 1957 has unleashed a new danger for north-lying countries: killer bees.

Killer bees? That's not a proper Doom.

Buzzzzz

ouCH!

Also called the Africanised honeybee, this species of insect is much more aggressive than the European variety and people who accidentally stray into their territory can be attacked savagely. The venom in the killer bee's sting isn't more powerful than that of ordinary honeybees. Their danger lies in the fact that they are more defensive and more ready to attack as a swarm. They are known to be capable of killing a grown man.

Formerly bred in the Central American tropics because of their higher honey productivity, bees from Africa have mated with native species and created this new and dangerous hybrid. Because they cannot survive harsh winters, their spread has been restricted to areas south of Texas. But as the climate warms, they have begun migrating, and have been found as far north as Chesapeake Bay, near Washington DC.

They've got attitude, and they're moving north at the rate of two kilometres a day.

c) Gulf Stream Disruption

Global warming makes us all get hotter, right?

Wrong.

Geophysicists worry that as the Earth heats up it will melt parts of the polar caps. As the cooler water flows southward from the North Pole, it might deflect the Gulf Stream, plunging Europe and northern parts of America into a new ice age.

The Gulf Stream is a huge conveyor of water from the Caribbean out into the Atlantic. Partway across, it divides and sends warmer seawater north to Canada and eastward to northern Europe. If it were not for this giant convection heater, temperatures would be as much as five degrees lower, making much of the densely populated region all but uninhabitable.

HAPPY MAP OF THE GULF STREAM

But the danger doesn't end there. As Bill McGuire, a geophysical hazards professor at University College, London, says, 'The possibility exists that a disruption of the Atlantic currents might have implications far beyond a colder northwest Europe, perhaps bringing dramatic climatic changes to the entire planet.'

It's all happened before. As recently as 10,000 years ago, during a cold period called the Younger Dryas, the Gulf Stream's force was about two-thirds of current levels, with a corresponding dip in European temperatures of up to ten degrees. All of which proves how little we know of the effects of climate change.

Turn up the temperature and freeze to death.

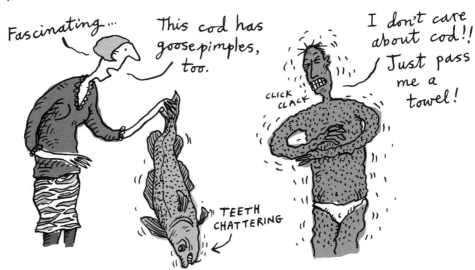

d) Hypercanes

Are super storms on their way?

A theoretical storm called a hypercane would have wind speeds of 500 miles per hour and could cover an area the size of North America. Based on what we know of its smaller cousins like Katrina, present levels of civilisation and most of the population would not be able to survive. Luckily, this supersize hurricane is only possible in extreme circumstances.

Yip!

Auntie Em?
Toto?

Like severe global warming.

Scientists calculate that ocean temperatures would have to rise some 15 degrees Celsius in order to produce such an event. That's a lot more than the 3.5 degrees considered possible at present, arising from projections of carbon emissions.

But however fervent a believer in man-made climate change you may be, that's not the only way the Earth gets hotter. Huge underground eruptions, being struck by an asteroid or comet and unusual solar activity could add to our own contributions.

Some meteorologists believe that Katrina was at least partly caused by global warming. They point out that the fuel of giant storms is the water vapour emerging from seas. What began as a category one storm in 2005 became a category five while idling over the warm waters of the Caribbean. By the time it hit the coast of Louisiana and Mississippi it had become the worst weather event in memory.

Some estimates say that the intensity of a hurricane can be predicted by knowing the sea temperature. A rise of 1.5 degrees above average would mean an additional 15–20% in wind speed and size. By that reasoning, a rise of 3.5 degrees would bring us storms of up to 50% more intensity, and they would happen more frequently. Add in some solar flares, an eruption or two and you have a recipe for disaster.

Maybe the storms wouldn't have winds of 500 miles an hour, but 300. And maybe they wouldn't be the size of North America.

Just the size of Texas.

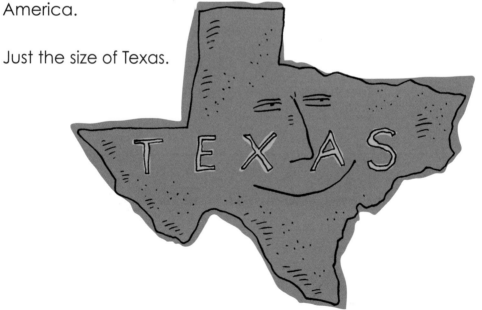

NOT ACTUAL SIZE. REAL TEXAS IS A BIT BIGGER. AND DOESN'T HAVE A FACE.

e) Endless Winter

Never mind global warming. What if summer was cancelled?

If something causes a dense enough blanket of smoke and ash to rise into Earth's upper atmosphere, scientists say that what will follow will be a rerun of the 'Year Without a Summer' of 1816. Following the eruption of Mount Tambora in Indonesia in 1815, Europe and North America were shrouded in a layer of smoke and ash so thick that temperatures dropped to unheard-of lows.

As far away as China, rice crops froze in the fields and water buffalo died. A dramatic increase in food prices and wide-spread starvation followed throughout the US and eastern Canada, and Welsh farmers travelled huge distances begging for food.

WHY NOT TRY THAT VOLCANIC ASH EXPERIMENT AGAIN?

You do, and I'll...

A resulting epidemic of typhus ravaged Ireland, with deaths thought to reach 100,000. There were food riots in Switzerland. Byron wrote his poem 'Darkness' during the lost summer of 1816.

There are at least seven known sites of 'mega-volcanoes' on Earth, any one of which would eclipse Mount Tambora. The rumblings in Iceland in 2010, which resulted in flight cancellations across a wide area, are thought to be just the beginning of a long series of eruptions of much greater intensity.

But it's not only volcanoes that can cause a drastic global temperature drop.

Nuclear winter is another possibility. For this to happen, it would not be necessary to see an all-out confrontation between the major nuclear powers. A local conflict such as sometimes

A NEW LIFE FORM EVOLVES

seems to threaten between India and Pakistan would do the job. The resulting famine and disruption of the world economy might account for more deaths than the bombs themselves.

Impact winter is the name given to the cloud of debris that would follow a strike by an asteroid or comet anywhere on Earth. The effects would be the same. Those who survived the high winds, tsunamis and blast radius of such an impact would face a lowering of global temperatures of up to 20 degrees. By contrast, the mercury in 1816 fell by less than one degree C.

Just when we thought the future was going to be too hot, we hear that we might freeze instead.

Robotic Revolt

Revolt of the robots? Artificially created intelligent machines controlling humanity for its own good? Isn't that just science fiction?

Not according to top cyber-scientists, who recently organised a hush-hush conference to discuss the possibilities of artificial intelligence. The conference was the brainchild of Eric Horvitz, principal researcher at Microsoft. Some scientists, like Alan Winfield, professor at the University of the West of England, feel that we are rapidly nearing a point where advances in artificial intelligence should be vetted, as in drug trials, as a protection against harm to humans.

Unmanned predator drones already operate in Afghanistan, programmed to search out and kill humans. Though these are at present controlled by people, they are rapidly moving towards complete autonomy. According to *The Sunday Times*, Samsung has developed

HOW TO ASSEMBLE YOUR OWN PERSONAL ROBOT NANNY

fig 1 ~

fig 2 ~
FIX PART A
TO PART B

fig 3 ~
FIX PART C
TO PART D

fig 4 ~
FIX PART E
TO PART F

fig 5 ~
FIX PART G
TO PART H

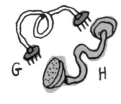

fig 6 ~
FIX PART I
TO PART J

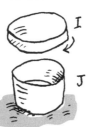

fig 7 ~
FIX ALL THE
BITS YOU'VE
MADE TOGETHER

fig 8 ~
NOW KEEP
GOING WITH
ALL THE
REST...

fig 9 ~ ...UNTIL YOU'RE DONE! SWITCH IT ON AND VOILA!

autonomous sentry robots, who can be programmed to shoot to kill.

Robots are already available who can learn their owner's behaviour, imitate their owner's voice and even recharge themselves when batteries run low. A variety of 'virus' robot can be inserted into mobile phones, enabling third parties to masquerade as the owners and penetrate bank accounts.

A new and potentially worrying element of artificial intelligence is known as 'swarm robotics', a system linking simple individual machines into a collective intelligence, like that of ants or bees. Linking up would make any cyber revolt ridiculously simple.

Whee!

Ring-a-ring-a-roses...

INDIVIDUALLY STUPID WASTE-PAPER-BASKET ROBOTS, WHEN LINKED TOGETHER, COMBINE INTO A GROUP INTELLIGENCE.

IF ONE MORE ROBOT JOINS THEY WILL EVOLVE INTO A WARRIOR TROOP.

HERE WE SEE THEM PERFORMING THEIR SINISTER DANCE.

Chillingly, an American firm is developing a 'nursebot' to replace or supplement human carers, designed to feign empathy with the patient.

Maybe they'll be smiling as they pull the trigger.

92

Genetic Engineering

Could we one day split into
two separate species?

This idea is one of the scariest that the GM-resisting lobby has
come up with. Since the breakthrough that cracked the
human genome, it has become clear that it is only a matter of
time before genetic engineering reaches into every corner of
biological existence. We know of the huge advantages such
science will bring: things like curing diabetes, creating
high-yielding food crops to cope with the growth in
population, and designing laboratory animals that more
closely resemble humans for drug trials.

But not everyone is convinced. While America cheerfully
produces GM crops for the table, the European Union has held
back. They are far from alone. But why?

Among the several nightmare scenarios that haunt the fearful,
two stand out. One is that we don't have sufficient knowledge
now (or perhaps ever) to know what it is we don't know. In one
imagined future, a hardly known disease reappears and
attacks an important food crop, such as rice. The original
strains of the plant may have had resistance to the virus, but
the GM version fails to anticipate this. The only recourse would
be to return to the original rootstock, but this will have
disappeared under a wave of optimistic genetic meddling.

Result: famine.

Another dire possibility has been proposed by reputable

FEEDING TIME

scientists. It involves the genetic mutation of humans, in order to produce 'designer babies'. These super-children would have higher intelligence, better looks, longer lives and much more raw talent. Because of the free market system, this 'germline' modification would only be affordable to the already rich. The poor would have to reproduce without any assistance, creating babies that in real terms are genetically inferior.

Molecular biologist Lee M. Silver has said that he can foresee a time when the gulf between the modified and 'natural' babies becomes so great that humanity actually divides into separate species.

This raises an even more frightening scenario. Our universal injunction against cannibalism applies only to members of the same species. Speaking globally, we don't mind eating cows, whales and even dogs.

Who's next?

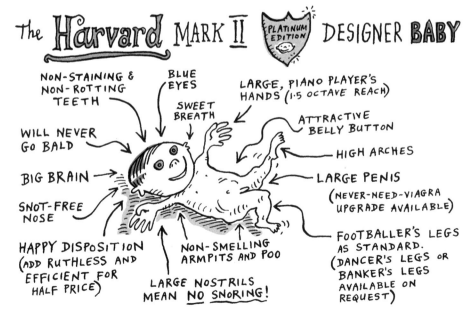

The Harvard MARK II [PLATINUM EDITION] DESIGNER BABY

NON-STAINING & NON-ROTTING TEETH

BLUE EYES

SWEET BREATH

LARGE, PIANO PLAYER'S HANDS (1·5 OCTAVE REACH)

ATTRACTIVE BELLY BUTTON

WILL NEVER GO BALD

HIGH ARCHES

BIG BRAIN →

LARGE PENIS
(NEVER-NEED-VIAGRA UPGRADE AVAILABLE)

SNOT-FREE NOSE

HAPPY DISPOSITION
(ADD RUTHLESS AND EFFICIENT FOR HALF PRICE)

NON-SMELLING ARMPITS AND POO

LARGE NOSTRILS MEAN NO SNORING!

FOOTBALLER'S LEGS AS STANDARD.
(DANCER'S LEGS OR BANKER'S LEGS AVAILABLE ON REQUEST)

Backwards Evolution

Is the human gene pool getting weaker?

Ever since William Shockley first used the term 'dysgenics' and caused dismay in the 1960s by claiming that stupider people had more babies, the notion that we are passing on weaker genes to each succeeding generation has gone underground. Studies have since shown that there is no connection between low IQ scores and number of progeny. The submerged racist nuances angered politicians and affected research grants. Its opposite, eugenics, has remained connected to Nazism and other fascist ideologies.

But since then we have entered an age of genetic science. Now there is a new way for 'desirable' and 'undesirable' traits to be passed on. Not by what used to be thought of as natural selection, but by manipulation in laboratories.

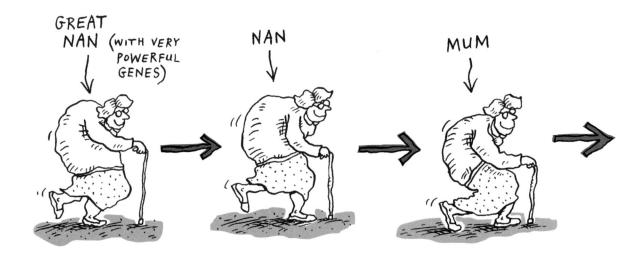

Meanwhile, medicine has developed treatments for diseases that would have been fatal in earlier times. A stroll through the graveyards reveals just how many people didn't survive conditions that are now easily managed.

But this blessing has a dark side. If more people survive who formerly wouldn't have, the diseases and disabilities that might have ended with them get passed on into the future. Scaremongers worry that these conditions may wind up affecting everybody in a few generations.

So it boils down to a race between inherited weaknesses and genetic fixes. A gamble involving 'weakness' vs genetically manipulated 'strength'.

Any takers?

Thanks to medical science saving her life and preserving her genes, now everyone in the world has my great nan's funny hips, bad back, crazy hair, obsession with Coronation Street and terrible dress sense.

ME (AGE 35)

COMPLETE RANDOM STRANGERS

ON AND ON INTO THE FUTURE...

Grey Goo

Self-replicating tiny machines that eat the Earth in one weekend.

1950s horror movie?

Hungry... Hungry... Hungry...

MAGNIFIED TEN BILLION TIMES

Not according to certain worried scientists, who foresee the future risks of nanotechnology. It has long been realised that one day microscopic robots may be made that can do such marvellous things as cleaning up oil spills and even removing carbon atoms from the atmosphere. The technology is still in its infancy, but signs are that this may become a possibility.

In early conceptions, 'nanobots' imitate the biological model. That is, they are tiny organisms that function in the same way as microorganisms. Not only would they perform the functions for which they were designed, they would make more and more copies of themselves.

In his 1986 book *Engines of Creation*, Eric Drexler calculated that in just ten hours an unchecked self-replicating auto-assembler would spawn 68 billion offspring; in less than two days the auto-assemblers would outweigh the Earth. The result would be that the entire planet would be reduced to a kind of 'grey goo'.

More recent statements from the scientific community have allayed some of these fears. The August 2004 Institute of Physics article by Drexler and Chris Phoenix says: 'Nanotechnology-based fabrication can be thoroughly non-biological and inherently safe: such systems need have no ability to move about, use natural resources, or undergo incremental mutation. Moreover, self-replication is unnecessary... Accordingly, the construction of anything resembling a dangerous self-replicating nanomachine can and should be prohibited.'

That's a relief then. Nothing to worry about. It will be prohibited.

Just like nuclear weapons.

DOOM SCENARIO:
MAD SCIENTIST DOOM

Electromagnetic Pollution

Invisible killer rays are all around us.

This sounds like fantasy fiction, but is rapidly becoming science fact. As our electronic gadgets become more and more sophisticated, we may find that we are trading convenience for safety.

Take mobile phones, for instance. The kind of radiation (EMF) found in these handy little wireless devices has long been a suspect in the search for causes of brain and eye cancer. The World Health Organisation has concluded that there is no direct causal link between the Big C and mobiles, but recommends limiting their use as a precaution. Others, such as Dr George Carlo, an epidemiologist, thinks that mobile phone radiation can be very dangerous. And he was heading a study funded by the big cellphone industry itself.

In addition to brain and eye cancer, some of the potential risks include DNA damage, an increase in the female hormone oestrogen (see pages 146–4), testicular cancer and loss of fertility, as well as a decrease in the effectiveness of anti-cancer drugs such as Tamoxifen. Because EMF may disrupt cognitive function, users can become confused while driving. One writer even compares the effects to alcohol intoxication.

Walking into lampposts while talking on your mobile hasn't so far appeared in the research as a potential hazard. Nor has having your private calls and texts hacked into or accidentally found by your partner, but these can also have unpleasant consequences.

Even keeping your mobile away from your head and groin won't offer total protection. We are subjected to something like 100 million times as much EMF as our grandparents. Health therapist Helen Adendorff compares it to being in a room full of heavy smokers, but without being able to leave or open the window.

They used to say that passive smoking was harmless, too.

...yes, let's meet.... 9 monday... no... yes...

Did you?...

I'd like one of the big ones... really big... please...

She kissed me... yeah... I know...

Swim, don't run...

Room 173...

I loved the new jumper...

Have you found your keys yet?

...give me your heart...

...meet you in the hotel...

...pretend I'm touching you...

I'm going to say something I might regret

I could eat you up...

IF WE COULD SEE ELECTROMAGNETIC RAYS...

Cyber Warfare

Everyone loves the Internet. It's a great way to buy things, keep in touch with your friends and look at pictures that used to be under the newsagent's counter. But now its ugly face has appeared.

Unknown enemies could use our own computers to destroy us.

ATTENTION!

IF YOU ARE READING THE DIGITAL EDITION OF THIS BOOK, THE AUTHORS ARE LOOKING OUT AT YOU RIGHT NOW FROM YOUR iPAD OR OTHER HANDHELD COMPUTER DEVICE.

BUZZ... CLICK... WHIRR...

IF YOU BOUGHT THE OLD-FASHIONED PAPER VERSION... HELLO! THIS PAGE IS PRINTED IN UP-TO-THE-MINUTE SMART INK™ INCORPORATING NANO CAMERA TECHNOLOGY, AND THE AUTHORS ARE SCRUTINISING YOU AS YOU READ. NICE SHIRT. PITY ABOUT THE HAIR.

Defence specialists think the threat of cyber attack is real. So much so, in fact, that the British Government is now listing it as one of the major threats to national security, alongside terrorist bombs.

As recently as five years ago, the concept of cyber attack hardly existed outside sci-fi novels. It was known that hackers had invaded certain classified websites from time to time, but this was considered to be little more than pranks on the part of teenage computer nerds.

A COMPUTER HACKER

No more all-night Call of Duty for you, Micron.

HACK!
CHOP!

Things have changed. A computer virus called Stuxnet recently penetrated the government cyber systems of Iran, Indonesia and India. More than 45,000 computers were infected or destroyed, including those that regulate Iran's burgeoning nuclear industry.

No one knows who the culprits are. The program is too expensive and sophisticated to have been built on a lone malcontent's laptop. It almost certainly has to be the effort of a country. The finger of blame is mostly levelled at Israel, because their relationship with Iran is the most fraught. But specialists think it could be America, Germany or even us.

If it is a national effort, Stuxnet represents the first shot in a war unlike any other in history. The prospect is so alarming that even the tight purse strings of the coalition government have been loosened in response. Some think that there are now four military services in the UK: army, navy, air force and GCHQ.

The fear is that cyber attack can do more than rob information and destroy computers. The sophistication of the new virus has made defence experts realise that enemy hackers could actually disrupt or disable real world services like water supplies, transport and electricity networks. But freezing in the dark isn't the worst possible nightmare. There's something even worse that could happen.

They could launch our missiles.

These politicians are BORING me to death...
SOCIAL & POLITICAL DOOM

The New Terrorism

I'm a terrorist.

But you look just like me!

Scare them to death.

What's the best way to defeat an enemy of overwhelming size and strength, using second-hand and home-made weapons? The answer is simple.

DANGEROUS JUNK

Terrorists have been around for a long time. Most of them follow a pattern. They feel that the status quo is invalid or illegal. Acts that would seem like despicable crimes in any other context are ennobled by the sense of shared purpose and struggle. It is the very horror of the acts that makes them most effective. Through the continuing fear of what they might do, they weaken and ultimately disable their enemies.

Civil liberties get eroded. Questionable activities such as waterboarding and 'extraordinary rendition' follow. Surveillance of citizens increases. And with each new level of suppression, new enemies are created. The spiral continues until the old system becomes brittle and collapses.

The present crop of terrorists follows this familiar pattern. But there are two important differences. One is that the dangerous junk lying around and easily found on the Internet is so much more deadly than in times past. Recipes for poisonous gas and instructions for making explosives are as near as one keyboard click away.

Radioactive materials ranging from spent reactor rods bought

76

on the black market to hospital waste brings the construction of a 'dirty bomb' into the reach of amateurs. It is conceivable that crude but effective nuclear devices can be bought or simply assembled. And if a nuclear-armed country such as Pakistan should be taken over by terrorist groups, a full range of doomsday weapons enter the picture. Even a small nuclear exchange might generate a cloud of dust and debris that would bring on a cataclysmic winter that didn't go away.

The second difference between current and past terrorists is what makes the use of these devices much more possible.

Suicide.

If you believe that dying in the process of blowing up innocents is not just an unfortunate outcome of a necessary act but a divine mission complete with heavenly rewards, you become nearly invincible to ordinary attacks. If dying is a pay-off and not a penalty, it's hard to imagine stopping you.

How can we fight the new terrorists when killing them only makes them happy?

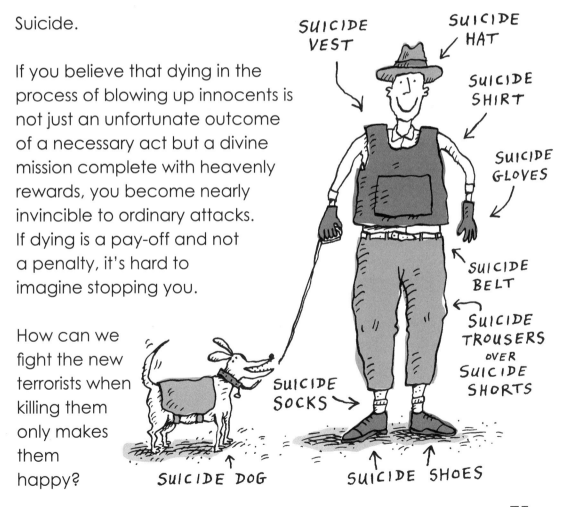

SUICIDE VEST

SUICIDE HAT

SUICIDE SHIRT

SUICIDE GLOVES

SUICIDE BELT

SUICIDE TROUSERS OVER SUICIDE SHORTS

SUICIDE SOCKS

SUICIDE DOG

SUICIDE SHOES

Nuclear War

Remember this one?

Children of the Cold War got used to the idea of living just a button press away from extinction. The Soviet bloc and the West bristled with ICBMs aimed at each other, with enough explosive power to destroy the Earth several times over. Only the fig leaf of Mutually Assured Destruction (MAD) lay between us and lights out. But that's all over now... Or is it?

With the collapse of the Soviet Union in the early 1990s the world took a deep breath. Treaties for gradual nuclear disarmament took effect, and lots of nukes were decommissioned with great fanfare. The accidental launch of missiles became less of a possibility. The weapons decreased in number, but they didn't go away.

The unstable new republics of the former USSR held some of the nuclear weapons within their territories. Rumours began to emerge of black market sales of radioactive materials and software. Western intelligence agencies had their hands full with tracking down missiles and warheads through the murky waters of new states we had never heard of.

Meanwhile, the proliferation of nuclear arms continued. India, Pakistan, China, Israel, North Korea – even South Africa, until they renounced them after the end of apartheid. Rumours surfaced that Saddam Hussein was close to developing an A-bomb. Now we know that Iran is bent on the rapid development of nuclear missiles. Some comfort is being taken from the fact that most of these states haven't yet produced a missile that can reach our shores. The numbers of nukes aren't that great yet, either. That means that any nuclear skirmish would be 'local' and over very quickly.

But the chilling truth is that any nuclear war anywhere would be capable of wiping us all out. If some suicidal fanatics take over the government of Pakistan, for instance, and launch a missile at Israel, they might as well draw a bead on London or New York. What would follow such an attack is the massive disruption of the global economy, freezing the exchange of food and energy, a storm of radioactive fallout that would encircle the globe, and a dense blanket of atmospheric dust that could cut out the Sun's light for years.

If the blast doesn't get you, the endless winter will.

MAD US
PRESIDENT
DOOM

Economic Meltdown

You can't do a lot about natural disasters, except try to cope.
If an asteroid has our name on it, that's outside our control.
If an unknown virus that lives in a species of bats in a
Madagascan cave suddenly mutates into a global
pandemic, all we can do is work to save ourselves with
science. But there's one looming doomsday scenario that
we can foresee, but not prevent. Something we're doing
ourselves.

Global economic collapse.

Depressions come and go like shuttle buses. They ebb and flow
within the limits of a worldwide economic system that
contains boom and bust years. They seem to average out,
and after a time of hardship, rejoin the orderly queue of a
system that is constantly growing
and improving. Sooner or later,
everyone benefits.

Where have all
the trees gone?

To be pulped and   Or so we believe.
made into bank notes.

But now some mainstream economists are joining the ranks of loony survivalists and Internet paranoids who predict the total collapse of the world economy. Ask any two of them how this might happen and you will get three answers. Some of the warning signs are things like China's metastasising economy, the rapid depletion of fossil fuels and scarcity of food crops, the sheer enormity of world debt and the spectre of runaway inflation.

A PIE CHART
SHOWING
THINGS To SPEND
MONEY ON

You can look at the current global economy as a chain letter. As long as you can sell stakes in some future pay-off to those below you on the chain, you'll do just fine. Maybe the chain grows at 3% per year, like the ideal national economy. But at some point the scheme reaches a point of saturation. People refuse to buy into what seems a rickety, top-heavy structure. The network of promises seem less and less likely.

HOW A CAPITALIST ECONOMY WORKS

70

One significant default by a major economy is like pulling one card from a card house.

What frustrates the idealists of the international marketplace is that economic boom and bust is down to a single, stubbornly resistant element: confidence. If the mood of the players is optimistic, things go humming along nicely. When things are overpriced and overleveraged, that's fine, as long as nobody spots the emperor's non-existent clothes.

But in a year when solar flares, shifting magnetic fields and unusual seismic activity have already made us uneasy, confidence starts to drain away. Instead of buying, people begin to save and hoard. As this activity deserts the market, things get worse. People lose their jobs. Countries erect trade barriers for self-protection, creating tension and skirmishing. As a currency wobbles, runs begin on banks. People store up foodstuffs and even ammunition in some places, and look suspiciously at their neighbours. In a full-blown financial panic, rioting, looting and civil collapse beckon.

Chaos.

But surely this couldn't happen here, you might think. Not in a civilised country with a long tradition of democratic stability. There must be laws in place. There must be some reasonable people in charge who know what to do. There are right-thinking, benevolent experts who know how to manage it all, aren't there?

Of course there are. The bankers.

Obesity Epidemic

Are you sitting comfortably while reading this book? Neither too hot nor too cold? Not feeling hungry?

The world's ending, I'll eat as much as I like!

You're killing yourself.

Being comfortable is making us some of the world's fattest and least healthy people. If we're not a bit cold or too hot because we rely on central heating and air conditioning we're not burning enough calories to stay fit, medics tell us. In 2010, more than 10,000 British people needed urgent hospitalisation because they were so fat that their lives were in immediate danger. And it's not just us at risk; nearly a third of our kids are overweight or obese. Doctors aren't mincing words: this is an epidemic.

It seems that if we live what we now think of as a 'normal' life, we're becoming prey to a whole catalogue of ailments, including diabetes, heart disease and some types of cancer. Everything we've ever achieved in terms of creature comforts has become a threat to our continued existence.

The labour-saving meals that line the supermarket shelves are laden with calories, fats and salt we cannot properly use. The machines that we longed for in the mid-20th century have begun to weaken and sicken us. The computer games and the fizzy drinks our children consume may well make their life-spans briefer than our own.

HOW TO HOLD AN END OF THE WORLD PARTY!

PANIC BUY LOTS OF DRINK, NIBBLES, CAKE, CHOCOLATE & SUGARY FOOD.

LOOT PAPER CUPS, STREAMERS, NAPKINS AND HATS.

HAVE A DRINK AND STUFF YOURSELF.

NO ELECTRICITY, SO MAKE YOUR OWN ENTERTAINMENT. SING SONGS WHILE PLAYING UKELELES.

DRINK UNTIL YOU CAN'T REMEMBER WHY YOU'RE PARTYING.

HOW TO HAVE AN END OF THE WORLD PARTY IF YOU'RE THIN

Wahoo.

EAT AND DRINK IMAGINARY FOOD

Paradoxically, the overfed live alongside the hungry. Obesity has recently become a problem even in so-called underdeveloped countries. As wealth improves, health risks multiply. Because fat and fashion don't mix, our young people are increasingly prone to malnutrition and severe eating disorders such as bulimia and anorexia nervosa.

With few exceptions, if you want to live a long and healthy life, you have to return to the modern equivalent of heavy toil and effort. That's why the gyms as well as the hospital wards are filling fast.

It's as if all the things we thought would make life easier and more enjoyable have conspired to finish us off. We're victims of our own success.

Be careful what you wish for.

Overpopulation

Do we need a second planet to survive?

Some scientists have warned that, at the current rate of population expansion, we will need a second planet by the middle of this century.

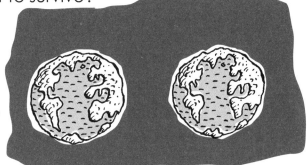

Until the beginning of the Industrial Revolution, Earth's population was fairly stable at about 250 million. We hadn't lost ground since the Black Death. But around the beginning of the 19th century, we started rapidly adding numbers, breaking the billion mark for the first time. By 1960 we had hit three billion, and in the next four decades we doubled that to six billion. We're now weighing in at 6.7 billion and counting. Even though the rate of increase has tailed off recently, most theorists believe that we will be living alongside ten to 11 billion others by 2050.

Estimates of maximum sustainable population vary, but some scientists are warning that we have already exceeded the level at which the planet can keep us all fed and watered. If the current population of the world ever manages to consume at the levels now enjoyed by Europe, we would need three times the available resources. Although most scientists agree that advances in technology may be able to keep abreast of the need for food, there are risks involved in turning the Earth into a 'giant human feedlot'. Species extinctions and environmental damage would be the certain consequences.

If we can't stop making new people, what can we do?

Cynics snarl that we needn't worry, because overpopulation will trigger wars, pandemics and famines and the planet will simply shrug off its excess inhabitants.

Optimists toil away in the laboratories for the perfect contraceptive. Some visionaries are actually working out ways to locate an empty planet somewhere in our galaxy and tow it into the solar system.

Maybe we could try cold showers?

THE PERFECT CONTRACEPTIVE —
A PORTABLE COLD SHOWER

Health & Safety

Imagine a world in which nothing bad could possibly happen to you. Where there was no danger of falling, being electrocuted, ingesting something fatal, being too hot or too cold or being infected by germs from someone else. Imagine a safer, kinder world, where gentle global rangers wearing Prozac smiles ensure that nothing we might ever do or ever wish to do could possibly bring harm or distress to ourselves or others.

Wouldn't that be wonderful?

The more advanced our civilisation becomes, the easier it is to predict and prevent danger. Comedy workmen used to fall from ladders or routinely smack each other's heads while carrying planks over their shoulders. Now hard hats make those routines impossible. It's safer, but a lot less funny. And new laws to protect us are being ground out in ever-increasing numbers.

Legislators, doctors, social workers and psychologists are working overtime to ensure that nothing bad can happen to you. Ever.

Doesn't that make you want to throw in the towel?

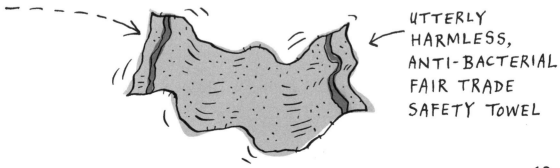

UTTERLY HARMLESS, ANTI-BACTERIAL FAIR TRADE SAFETY TOWEL

61

Religious Doom

When it comes to foretelling Doom, no one can compete with the world's religions.

The sheer variety of coming destruction in the holy books would make the most pessimistic of scientific doomsayers tremble. But, ominously, many of these Doom scenarios closely resemble the current worst-case speculations of the scientists.

In Islam, the world is hit by such huge earthquakes that the 'body of the Earth is broken'. One in the east, one in the west and one in what must seem like the centre of the world, the Arabian Peninsula. The sun will rise in the west, too, which sounds like a complete polar reversal. All the non-believers will die before winding up in hell, but the righteous will just get head colds.

The Christian version is best represented by some lines in the Book of Matthew, who says that the end will be a 'great tribulation, such as was not [seen] since the beginning of the world'. It will happen so suddenly that anyone who happens to be standing on his roof is warned not to go downstairs to get his things. He says those who are pregnant or breastfeeding will have it the worst, which suggests the possibility of nuclear fallout. He also tells us we should hope our flight from danger is not on the Sabbath, when you're not meant to do anything much.

Matthew even tells us how to recognise when the time is getting near. He says 'nation shall rise against nation, and there shall be famines and pestilences and earthquakes' in many places. That sounds a lot like where we are now, doesn't it?

But things get even worse. Immediately 'after the tribulation of those days shall the sun be darkened, and the moon shall not give her light, and the stars shall fall from heaven, and the powers of the heavens shall be shaken'.

In all the 'Abrahamic' faiths, the believers – also known as the 'righteous' – get saved. The Muslims get taken to heaven by Allah. The Christian 'elect' survive the cataclysm and, similarly to the Jews, are escorted by a Messiah to a new version of the Earth.

Everyone else is toast.

And that means YOU, reader.

Even the mild-mannered Buddhists weigh in with a nightmarish prediction of the Earth heating up, going dry and finally exploding. As far back as 500 BCE, global warming was an issue. The Buddha apparently thought this was a good idea, as it helped his followers see the world as something to be transcended.

So who's right?

Since the holy books agree that the faithful are saved and everyone else is condemned or destroyed, that means hell is going to be crowded.

If you take just the Mediterranean, for example, you've got hundreds of millions of people who are nominally Christian on one side, and hundreds of millions more on the other who are mostly Muslims. If either of their holy books is accurate, the better part of the population of the other side is in big – call it eternal – trouble.

Take your pick.

Holy War

There's another possibility for Doom that arises not from external sources, but from religion itself.

Every once in a while, human beings get all worked up about religious ideas. At present, we've got the brand of Islam known as Wahhabism, a fundamentalist version of the Sunni branch. This was the root of Osama bin Laden's holy war against virtually everyone who didn't agree with him.

But he's not alone. There are groups who define themselves as Christians who are infected with the same malady of absolutism, and who aren't above blowing up abortion clinics and shooting medics. Some of these True Believers are known to be awaiting the great war on the Plain of Armageddon, when the troops of the Antichrist (Muslims, Jews, Catholics, atheists – everyone except your own lot) are finally defeated.

If you too closely identify with what you consider the only truth, you begin to despise people who don't agree with you. This can bring about things like the Orthodox vs Roman Catholic split in the Balkans, the slaughter in Sri Lanka, and – oh yes – don't forget Northern Ireland.

When cultural change happens too rapidly, when economies get depressed, when confusion seems to be the state of just about everybody, that's when you start looking around for a new saviour. There often seems to be one handy. Then you're just one step away from guns and sexy uniforms. And Holy War.

Yippee!

WHICH RELIGION WILL REWARD YOU WITH EVERLASTING LIFE FOR ALL ETERNITY IF YOU TAKE THEIR SIDE FOR ARMAGEDDON?

BE SURE TO CHOOSE CORRECTLY...

53

Philosophical Doom

It is clear from reading the great philosophers that your existence isn't just nasty, brutish and short – it's an illusion.

You don't exist.

To prove it, try answering this little philosophical riddle:

If a tree falls in the forest, and there is no one to hear it, does it make a sound?

That question was first posed in the 18th century by George Berkeley, and it's been a big hole in the socks of philosophers ever since. Berkeley was a 'subjective idealist', meaning that in order for something to have an existence, it must be seen and noted by someone. His words, in Latin, naturally, were *'Esse est percipi'* or 'To be is to be perceived'.

You can't disprove that argument. You can just take it or leave it. The noise a falling tree makes needs an ear to hear it before it can come into existence.

If Berkeley was right, then we are not 'discovering' new galaxies with our telescopes, we are creating them. Without an observer, they wouldn't exist at all. If you're born, live and die without anyone ever seeing you, you've never existed.

Berkeley's day job was being a bishop, so he found a way around all this. He said that the noise made by the falling tree did exist, because God heard it. Of course, proving the existence of God is a lot more complicated than looking around in the woods for missing decibels.

So what does this have to do with Doom?

Doomsday might be next week or not, but everyone agrees on one thing: sometime in the next five billion years, our Sun will become a supernova, instantly eradicating us, our descendants, and any trace that we ever existed. Nothing will remain. No record, no monuments, no memories, no witnesses.

It will be as if we never were.

In fact, according to Berkeley's logic, it *will* be that we never were.

Sometimes Doom can come to an individual without the need for earthquakes, pandemics or gamma rays. Victims can be seen cowering in the background in our cities and towns, avoiding daylight and flinching from all human contact. These unfortunates are living, but utterly without hope.

This is **Personal Doom**, which can strike without warning and leave you wishing for something as relatively mild as global destruction.

Read on, if you dare.

No one has phoned me, emailed or sent me a text message ALL DAY.

SILENT

i — My skin is turning dry and blotchy!

ii — There are brown spots on the backs of my hands!

iii — I've got wrinkles and hairs on my upper lip!

And in my nose!

iv — My pores are HUGE!

v — My hair is dull and lifeless!!

vi — My thighs are like the skin of an orange!

And I've got varicose veins!!

vii — My ears are getting bigger! My breath smells! My feet hurt!

viii — End of the world in 15 minutes!

Thank God! Now no one will notice all the things that are wrong with me.

47

Sexual Ruin

Sex is liberating!

Sex must be constrained!

Sex is for continuing the human race.

CONFUSING, ISN'T IT?

Of course you're safe from sexually transmitted diseases. Like all sensible people, you rely upon monogamy, or at least take precautions.

But the bugs are getting cleverer.

NEW SEXUAL DISEASE BACILLIS

Ha ha ha ha...

He he he he he...

A plague that begins as a malaise of green monkeys in Africa can pop up in singles' bars in San Francisco. The epidemic of syphilis that shook Europe in the16th century was probably imported from the Americas by a few randy seamen, and nobody saw it coming.

Viruses, bacteria, fungi and parasites keep changing shape. They might well be evolving in ways the laboratories can't foresee. The bugs aren't in a hurry. They have lots of time.

Do we?

46

THIS NEW SEXUAL DISEASE BACILLIS CAN CHEW THROUGH CONDOMS

BELCH!

AND HERE'S ANOTHER WHICH CAN BE TRANSMITTED BY KISSING OR EVEN JUST TOUCHING A BREAST

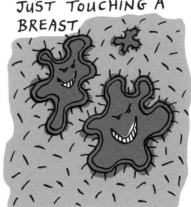

THIS ONE IS CONTRACTED BY MERELY THINKING ABOUT SEX

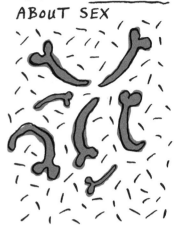

BUBBLE OF COMPLACENCY

These new STDs are alarming...

But we're ok, aren't we, darling, being married and monogamous and so on.

Of course we are, darling.

BEEP BEEP BEEP

A TEXT MESSAGE ARRIVES FROM HIS LOVER

Cooee!

BRIAN
DAVE
SID
SUE
FRANK
EZRA
HELEN
CHRISTOPH

WOMAN
DRIVEN BY THE INSTINCTS TO REPRODUCE AND CUDDLE.

MAN
DRIVEN BY THE INSTINCTS TO SPREAD HIS SEED, HAVE FUN DOING IT, PLUS TEMPTATION FROM THE DEVIL.

REAL WORLD

P.T.O.

45

TO JAPAN
TO ITALY
CHARDONNAY
WING PI
SUKI
SOFIA
HANK
BRIAN
BOB
TED
Toot toot!
DAVE
SID
Pixies
MOHOLY
FRANKIE
SUE
Coochie coo!
CHRISTOPH
HELEN
MISS STICKLER
SANDY
TO DENMARK
TO INDIA
TO BRAZIL

43

SOME MORE PERSONAL DOOM MOMENTS

42

ADD SOME OF <u>YOUR OWN</u> PERSONAL DOOMS HERE:

___ ___ ___ ___ ___ ___   ___ ___ ___ ___ ___
___ ___ ___ ___ ___ ___   ___ ___ ___ ___ ___
___ ___ ___ ___ ___ ___   ___ ___ ___ ___ ___

___ ___ ___ ___ ___ ___   ___ ___ ___ ___ ___
___ ___ ___ ___ ___ ___   ___ ___ ___ ___ ___
___ ___ ___ ___ ___ ___   ___ ___ ___ ___ ___

___ ___ ___ ___ ___ ___   ___ ___ ___ ___ ___
___ ___ ___ ___ ___ ___   ___ ___ ___ ___ ___
___ ___ ___ ___ ___ ___   ___ ___ ___ ___ ___

HERE'S A PERSONAL DOOM THAT WILL BE FAMILIAR TO MANY

ONE FORM OF PERSONAL DOOM IS REALISING THAT...

My life is meaningless.

I have no purpose.

I am utterly insignificant in the grand scheme of things.

I am as insignificant as this tiny spider.

?

Actually, I'm a great deal MORE significant than you.

I may play only a tiny role in the global network of living creatures, but at least I PLAY a role by helping to balance the ecology of the planet.

You, on the other hand, merely mess the planet up!

SQUISH! STAMP!

Ha. Who's the more significant one now?

INADEQUATE CHILDREN DOOM

METAPHORICAL DOOM

LITERAL DOOM

Getting a spot on my wedding day would be the end of the world!

Do We Love Doom?

The unmistakable lure of Doom raises all sorts of questions about us. Surely we can't enjoy contemplating a terrible end to ourselves and all we cherish.

Can we?

You might as well suppose that we don't love horror movies or being tossed about by scary rides at theme parks. That we avoid the gory details of crimes in thrillers. Or that we scrupulously stay away from any risks to our safety, such as hang-gliding or rock climbing.

After all, what we really want is to be safe, secure and happy.

Isn't it?

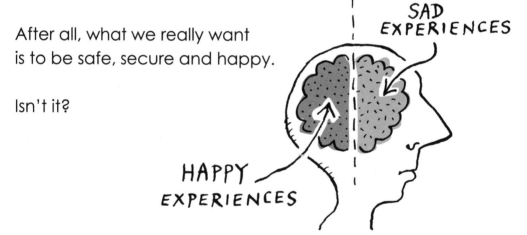

SAD EXPERIENCES

HAPPY EXPERIENCES

Let's imagine that in the future our descendants have perfected a way of completely separating their lives into relentlessly happy and consistently unhappy compartments.

They do this by separating each individual – at birth – into two clones.

i-

ii-

These identical people go through life side by side, one person experiencing only the comfortable, happy and pleasurable things in his – or her – life, the other living only the anxious, unpleasant and painful moments.

Meet David Jones and David Jones.

The Joneses are a successful man with a good income, a lovely home and a beautiful wife, Jane.

JANE JONES

David Jones – let's call him Jones 1 and Jones 2 – has had his fair share of good and bad experiences.

Jones 1 had a completely happy childhood.

Jones 2 had a miserable one.

Jones 1 was
applauded
at school and
did well.

Jones 2
struggled
and was bullied.

Jones 1 cuddles
and coos with his
lovely wife...

...while Jones 2
argues, slams
doors and
smashes things.

One morning the police are called to the Jones home, where they find that David Jones has hanged himself in the garage.

David Jones stands silently nearby.

The mystery the police must solve is this:

Which David Jones couldn't take it any longer and killed himself?

Someday you're going to die. Whether it's in a comfy bed, surrounded by grieving relatives, or under the wheels of a number 11 bus, the result is the same. One day it will be all over.

So why is Doom any different? If you die alone or with 6.2 billion other people, isn't the result identical?

DOOM vs DEATH

ONE OF THESE TWO PEOPLE HAS JUST BEEN TOLD THEY ARE ABOUT TO DIE. THE OTHER HAS LEARNT THAT THE WORLD IS COMING TO AN END. CAN **YOU** TELL WHICH IS WHICH?

Aaargh!!

HINT~

DEATH IS THE PREDICTABLE END OF YOURSELF.

DOOM IS THE END OF HISTORY, THE FUTURE, MEMORY AND HOPE.

29

A Glimmer of Hope

Some Certain Dooms that Haven't Happened (so far)

BONK BONK BONK BONK BONK BONK BONK...

FALSE
ALARM
CLOCK

a) Man-made Black Holes

Before the Large Hadron Collider at the European Organization for Nuclear Research (CERN) started shooting protons around its 17-mile tunnel in 2008, panicky stories began to appear in the press. While earnest scientists looked for a theoretical quantum particle called the Higgs boson, laymen braced themselves for the emergence of small black holes that would metastasise and gobble up the Earth.

Black holes are mass compressed into such a small space that they swallow up everything they touch, including light. Around these is an area called the 'event horizon', which is the point of no return for anything unlucky enough to come into a black hole's powerful gravitational field. It has been compared to canoeing upstream away from a waterfall. At some point, you take the fall.

It made a perfect scenario for both pseudo-scientific cyber geeks and for religious doomsayers. The science buffs had the theoretical possibility of black holes, while the prophets of apocalypse were animated by the Higgs boson's nickname.

The God particle.

They're still firing subatomic particles under a Swiss mountain,

but so far we haven't been attacked by black holes. Meanwhile, some Chinese physicists have built a 'black-hole generator' out of copper wire in a disk that seems to suck up all known radiation, including light. It has several possible applications for industry. It will collect solar heat better than anything we now have, which is good news for our alternative energy plans.

It may also defeat radar screens, making it possible to fly warplanes into someone else's airspace undetected.

Which is bad news for all of us.

b) The Millennium Bug

The coming of the Third Millennium threw up a predictable number of end-of-the-world scares, but one in particular seized the imagination of scientists, politicians and business leaders. This was called the Y2K Problem or the Millennium Bug.

Because most computers used only the last two digits of a date in their calculations, it was widely feared that the machines that run our civilisation would either stop working altogether or else chuck us all backwards to 1900.

Anticipating disaster, big corporations spent millions on technicians to fiddle with their digital equipment. Some banks suspended the operation of swipe cards three days before the new year actually came in. Horror scenarios abounded: looting, air crashes, economic collapse and the unintentional launch of nuclear missiles.

SOME DATES TO WORRY ABOUT:

No 1 ~ TOMORROW

A Horseman of the Apocalypse! RUN!!

Calm down, Stewart. It's only little Judy practising for the gymkhana.

YOWL!

YIP!

24

When the day actually came, nothing much happened.

In the United States, a hundred slot machines at several race tracks in Delaware stopped working. Bus ticket machines packed up in two Australian states. A French meteorological channel showed a nonsense date on one of its weather maps.

The computers, it seemed, were either too smart to be fooled or too dumb to notice.

That should sort things out for the next century or so, you might think. Unfortunately, many computer specialists predict it might happen again in 2038. That's because the original Unix timestamp stores a date and time as a 32-bit integer, counting the number of seconds since 1 January 1970. After 2038, this number will be too large to be contained in 32 bits. Some computer applications are already switching to 64-bit systems to head this off.

Sorry, Mrs Thumbtack, but I'm the DIGITAL horseman and it's time to vaporise your BANK ACCOUNTS!

SNORT

But if any of the other things in this book come to pass, we probably won't have to worry about 2038 anyway.

SOME THINGS WHICH WILL BE GONE FOREVER

The sparkle of sunlight on water.

Children's voices in the bright air.

The smell of cut grass on a summer's day.

Summer.

Also Autumn, Winter and Spring.

Woodsmoke curling up into a still evening.

The scratchy feeling of wool on bare skin.

The anticipation of a good meal.

The smell of freshly brewed coffee.

The sun rising over the sea.

The splash of a fish in a limpid pool.

The cries of lovers.

Frost on a car windscreen.

Car windscreens.

Cars.

Afternoon tea and hot buttered crumpets.

The warm breath of a dog.

The honk of a vast juggernaut.

TOOT!

The taste of fried food.

The smell of a fresh baby.

SNIFF

Waking in a warm bed and drifting off to sleep again.

Mmm...

Snowballs.

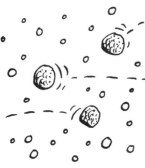

The ideas contained in books.

Books — like this one.

Phew. Thank goodness this book will be gone. It's making me feel rather low.

21

DWELLING ON DOOM CAN BECOME A BIT DEPRESSING, SO WHY NOT DISTRACT YOURSELF BY MAKING THIS ATTRACTIVE

STRAW TO CLING ON TO?

SIMPLY:

i ~ CUT ALONG THE SOLID LINES.

ii ~ ROLL STRAW AROUND A PENCIL.

iii ~ APPLY GLUE TO TAB A.

iv ~ PRESS TAB A TO TAB B UNTIL SET.

v ~ CLUTCH FINISHED STRAW TIGHTLY UNTIL DOOM TAKES PLACE.

That's much better...

NOT TOO TIGHTLY! BE CAREFUL NOT TO CRUSH IT.

TAB B UNDER HERE

TAB A ~ COVER WITH GLUE

ROLL

20

SEARCHING FOR A LOOPHOLE*

According to quantum theory there are an infinite number of parallel universes. Surely not ALL of them will end in DOOM?

I'm afraid the others already did. This is the last universe.

THE END IS NOW

* Unlike a BLACK HOLE, a LOOPHOLE is not recognised as a true scientific term. A LOOPHOLE is merely a legal, political or economic term.

HOW WORRIED ARE YOU?

Scientists tell us that, whatever happens, the Earth is going to end when the Sun becomes a supernova in about five billion years. So why aren't we bothered?

At what point do you start getting worried? Put a tick next to the first date when things will begin to alarm you.

☐ 1 BILLION YEARS — zzzzzzzzzz...

☐ 1 MILLION YEARS — YAWN...

☐ 1 THOUSAND YEARS — Doesn't affect me.

☐ 100 YEARS — Relax. You'll be 105.

☐ 10 YEARS — Better get on with having some fun. Honey, cancel our retirement policy!

☐ 1 YEAR — This is getting SERIOUS!

☐ NEXT WEEK — I wonder what life is really all about? And who would have won the FA cup?

☐ NOW! — AAAAAARGH...

WHAT TO TELL YOUR CHILDREN
SOME USEFUL & EMPTY DENIALS & REASSURANCES

I'll protect you, darling.

Nothing bad will happen while I'm here.

The scientists will come up with something.

Don't believe everything you see on TV.

They invent new medicines every day.

It'll be all right in the morning.

Everything is going to be ok...

HOW DOOM MIGHT HAPPEN...

i – INSTANTLY AND WITHOUT WARNING.

It might happen before I reach the end of this sentence...

Or me this one...

ii – QUICKLY, BUT AFTER A LONG BUILD-UP.

Plenty of time to chat while we're waiting.

I'll get my novel finished, too.

iii – SLOWLY, OVER MONTHS AND YEARS.

I've run out of things to say.

Thank God.

iv – ANTICLIMACTICALLY.

Aw... I thought it would be a HUGE bang.

It's more of a fizzle...

PSSST...

PSSSST...

PSSST...

v – INSIDIOUSLY.

vi – RELIGIOUSLY.

vii – WITH IRRITATINGLY BAD TIMING.

viii – SURPRISINGLY.

15

Doom is a great time to discover your deep beliefs. Here are some sample responses by people with different points of view. Which one matches yours?

The Stoic: 'Well, what did you expect?'

The Born Again: 'Rapture should be along any minute now.'

The New Ager: 'We're just moving to a higher level of vibration.'

The Meditator: 'OM.'

The Holy Book Thumper: 'You were warned.'

The Optimist: 'Maybe this is a fresh start.'

The Mystic: 'Those gamma rays are really the wings of the Spirit.'

The Hedonist: 'Let's get naked.'

The Pew Sitter: 'Quick, someone play "Abide with Me".'

The Scientologist: 'If only I'd paid enough to get to the next level.'

The Agnostic: 'Will somebody please explain what's happening?'

The Atheist: 'Bugger...'

POSITIVE DOOM THERAPY

COMPARED TO IMPENDING GLOBAL DOOM, ALL YOUR PERSONAL PROBLEMS WILL MELT INTO INSIGNIFICANCE.

I'll never have to go to work ever again!

I won't be lonely in my old age!

Worrying about the pointlessness of life now seems pointless...

I don't have to worry about having no pension.

Or paying the bills.

I don't have to watch any more reality TV.

Or read a newspaper.

My oedipal issues concerning my father are gone!

← TRANSVESTITE

No need to give up smoking — or go to the gym.

I can stop worrying about money.

All in all, DOOM's the therapy for me!

CHEERS!

I can continue to ignore all the unresolved issues concerning my sexuality.

I don't have to mend the fence or decorate the kitchen.

13

THE ETIQUETTE OF DOOM

SHOULD YOU RUSH ABOUT PUSHING AND SHOVING AND SCREAMING, OR WAIT PATIENTLY IN AN ORDERLY QUEUE FOR DOOM TO HAPPEN? ISN'T THE ANSWER OBVIOUS?

BE DIGNIFIED

SMILE STOICALLY

DON'T FORGET SOME TASTEFUL MAKE-UP

REMEMBER TO SHAVE

BRUSH YOUR HAIR & TRIM YOUR EYEBROWS

PLAY SOMETHING JOLLY ON YOUR INSTRUMENT

KEEP YOUR UPPER LIP STIFF

AND IF YOU DON'T PLAY AN INSTRUMENT START TAKING LESSONS

DON'T FORGET DEODORANT AT THIS SWEATY TIME...

WEAR NICE CLOTHES. DON'T LET YOURSELF GO. REMEMBER TO IRON EVERYTHING ~ IT'S IMPORTANT TO KEEP UP APPEARANCES AT A TIME LIKE THIS.

AND CLEAN UNDERWEAR

REMEMBER

IF THERE'S TIME, GET YOUR SUIT CLEANED

WAX YOUR LEGS!

ALWAYS SAY 'PLEASE' AND 'THANK YOU' AND TREAT OTHERS AS YOU WOULD LIKE TO BE TREATED. GOOD MANNERS COST NOTHING, EVEN WHEN THE WORLD IS ENDING.

POLISH YOUR SHOES

WHAT TO WEAR

SOMETHING SMART AND DRESSY...

... OR JUST SOME OLD, COMFORTABLE THINGS YOU DON'T MIND GETTING RUINED?

A PRACTICAL COLOUR WHICH WON'T SHOW MARKS AND STAINS WOULD BE SENSIBLE.

IDEALLY YOU WANT TO LOOK ATTRACTIVELY CRUMPLED WHILE STILL APPEARING EFFORTLESSLY IN CONTROL.

11

SOME WAYS TO SPEND YOUR LAST

24 HOURS ON EARTH...

Disaster Grab Kit

Lots of people are assembling little bags called Grab Kits, 72-hour kits and GOOD (Get Out Of Dodge) bags. You can even buy these from online shops specialising in survivalist supplies for anything up to a few hundred pounds. The deluxe models contain things like food and water for three days, light-weight tents and emergency blankets – even portable toilets.

When Doom strikes, if it is one of the slower models, you might wish to survive for a few days while it really gets going. So, what to pack?

HERE'S BEAUJOLAIS BROWN, 16:

whatever.

SPOT CREAM

MAKE-UP

CONDOMS

MOBILE

SHADES

TIGHTS

iPod

BREATH MINTS

SHOES

HARIBO

LIPSTICK

FAGS

VEST

WARM COAT

No way, Mum!

CHEWING GUM

DEPILATORY CREAM

AND HERE'S CYRIL BROWN, BEAUJOLAIS' DAD:

Your Own Grab Kit

Use this page to make a list of all the essentials you will need to survive out in the open, fight off cannibals and make that last, desperate trek to a high, defensible place with a clean water supply. We've filled in the first few to get you started.

1 Bag – to put it all in.

2 Sledge (in case of endless winter)

3 _____

4 _____

5 _____

6 _____

7 _____

8 _____

9 _____

10 _____

12 _____

13 _____

14 _____

15 _____

16 _____

17 _____

18 _____

19 _____

20 _____

21 _____

22 _____

23 _____

24 _____

25 In case all else fails – Rope.

Topicality Disclaimer

The authors realise that since this book went to press there will undoubtedly have been many new and terrifying Doom scenarios. In order to keep the book up to date, please list them below.

1 _____

2 _____

3 _____

4 _____

5 _____

6 _____

7 _____

8 _____

9 _____

10 _____

11 _____

Continue on a separate sheet if necessary

The Meaning of Doom

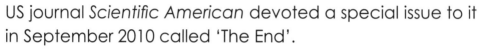

Everybody seems to be
thinking about the end of
the world these days.
So much so that the prestigious
US journal *Scientific American* devoted a special issue to it
in September 2010 called 'The End'.

It's not just the rash of Hollywood disaster-film producers and
pulp-fiction writers who exploit a widespread and growing
anxiety about doomsday. Nor is it only the usual Internet
alarmists who feed upon a melange of prophesies and
astrological signs and portents.

It's all of us.

Doomsday has been predicted dozens of times in our
written and oral history. So far, every one of these predictions
has turned out to be a false alarm. As the 20th century came
to an end, the scientists and politicians became convinced
that adding two zeros to the date would send computers into
freefall and bring about the total collapse of civilisation. The
'Y2K' phenomenon provided short-term employment to a few
cyber boffins, but 1 January 2000 came and went without
a single crash.

This should have been at least somewhat reassuring. Dismissed
as millenarian hysteria and consigned to history. But instead
we began to hear new voices crying, 'The sky is falling!' These
voices are from the scientific community itself. Even such
illustrious sources as Sir Martin Rees, Astronomer Royal, add to

the anxiety. According to *Scientific American*, he has offered a standing bet that up to one million people will die as the result of a biological catastrophe before 2020. The fact that earlier predictions such as that of the economist Thomas Malthus (1766–1834), who foresaw that population growth would inevitably be checked by mass starvation, and later the seeming certainty of destruction offered by the nuclear arms race, haven't brought about the apocalypse doesn't make any difference. We know Doom is approaching. Don't we?

① IMAGINE THIS BUTTON WILL DESTROY THE WORLD.

② PRESS IT.

③ FEELS GOOD, DOESN'T IT?

④ PRESS IT AGAIN.

As soon as one Doom scenario passes harmlessly by, we select another. If an asteroid misses us by a cosmological country mile, we begin to fret about solar flares. If swine flu turns out to be less than a biblical plague, we turn our attention to diseases like Ebola.

We seem to need Doom. But why?

No one is sure, but theories float to the surface. One easy answer is that worrying about the end of civilisation is somehow more comforting than facing the fact of our own personal Doom awaiting us in some distant hospital bed or roadside. It's exciting, where death is simply depressing. According to this theory, it's almost like the displacement of anger, as when being criticised by your boss makes you kick your dog.

Another theory is that it makes us feel important. The idea that we are living in exceptional times makes things less pedestrian. When we go to disaster movies and watch giant waves devouring cities, or super viruses laying waste to whole countries, we do so with relish. Being in, as Rees put it, 'our final century', adds glamour to a world made dull with taxes and telemarketing calls.

But there's a third possibility.

As *Scientific American* points out, we are creatures of the savannah, programmed over thousands of years to see patterns and trends in a multitude of events. As sociologist John R. Hall has said, 'If the world appears to be going to hell . . . maybe that's just what is happening.' As part of our basic survival equipment, we may be gifted with a kind of intuition that looks at things as they happen and makes predictions based on the emerging pattern. In other words, we may be right.

Woof!
Woof!
Woof!
Woo
Woo
Woo
Woo
Woo
Woo
Woo
Woo...

Dogs bark before earthquakes, don't they?

WHAT CAN WE DO
TO PREVENT IT?

TURN THE PAGE TO FIND OUT...

zero

Touchscreen Interactive Index

Use your eyes to scan this page until you locate a subject which interests you. Next, touch the subject with your fingertip to be transported instantly to the page you require.

Alternatively, if you are using the old-fashioned, economy, paper edition, select a subject using your eyes as described above, then memorise the page number. Next, insert your finger between two pages and manually lift and turn. Repeat until correct page is reached.

AFTER...

NOTHIN